AMERICA the BEAUTIFUL

SOUTH CAROLINA

By Deborah Kent

Consultants

George C. Rogers, Jr., Ph.D., Distinguished Professor Emeritus, Department of History, University of South Carolina

Rodger E. Stroup, Chief Curator, South Carolina State Museum

Robert L. Hillerich, Ph.D., Bowling Green State University, Bowling Green, Ohio

ↂ CHILDRENS PRESS ®
CHICAGO

A farm in the Piedmont

Project Editor: Joan Downing
Associate Editor: Shari Joffe
Design Director: Margrit Fiddle
Typesetting: Graphic Connections, Inc.
Engraving: Liberty Photoengraving

Library of Congress Cataloging-in-Publication Data

Kent, Deborah.
    America the beautiful. South Carolina.

    Includes index.
    Summary: Introduces the geography, history,
government, culture, recreation, and people of the
Palmetto State.
    1.   South Carolina—Juvenile
literature.   [1.   South Carolina.]   I.   Title.
F269.3.K46   1989   975.7   89-858
    ISBN 0-516-00486-7

An outdoor art
class along
Meeting Street
in Charleston

TABLE OF CONTENTS

Chapter 1

OLD SOUTH, NEW SOUTH

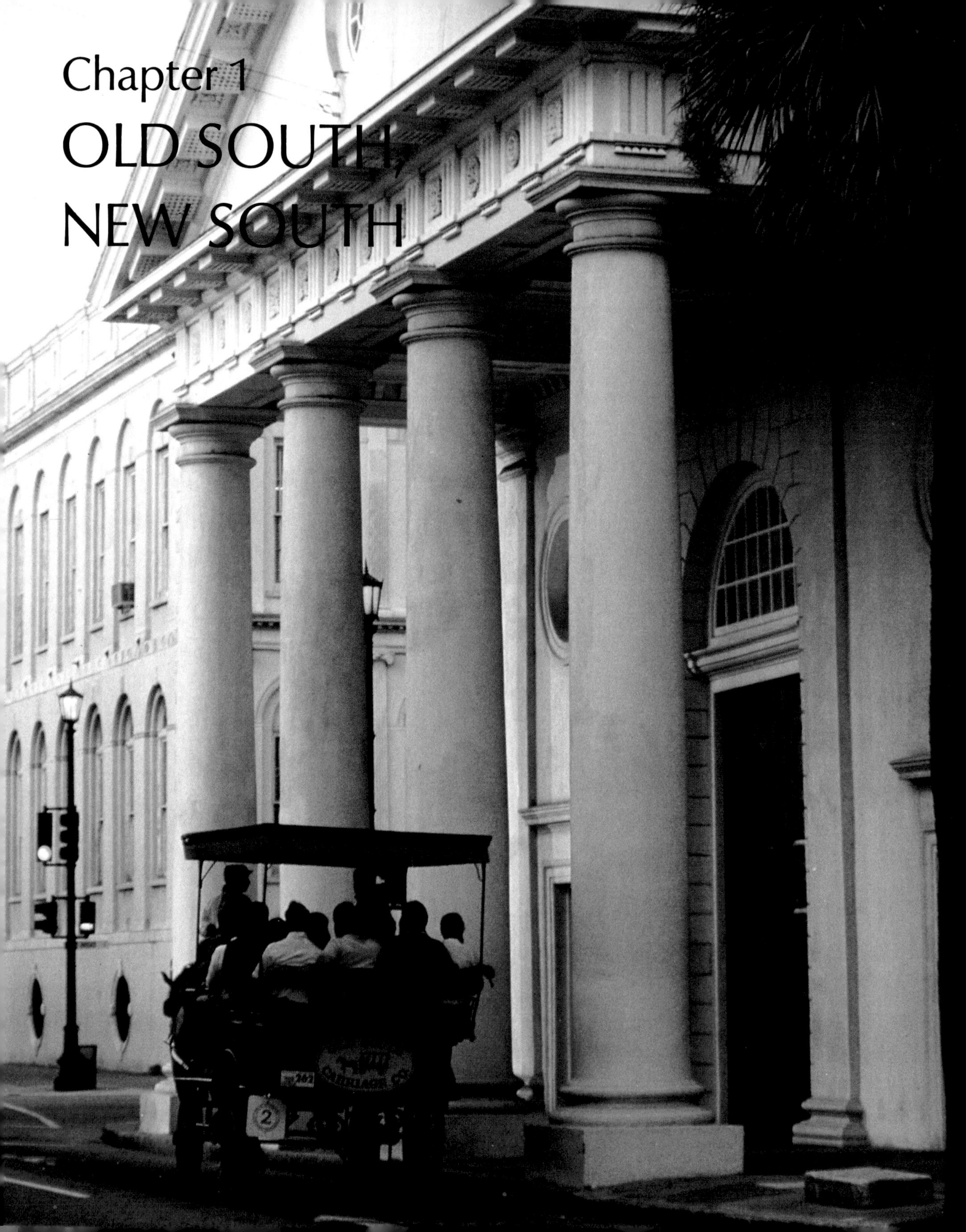

OLD SOUTH, NEW SOUTH

"Who were your people? Where does your family come from?" These are questions that South Carolinians often ask each other when they first meet. Many homes display the cherished portraits of great-grandparents and great-great-grandparents on the walls. Libraries and museums throughout the state contain extensive genealogical archives where families may burrow back to their roots.

The past holds a special fascination for South Carolinians, and family history makes the past real and personal. Most South Carolinians are descendants of the Europeans and Africans who first opened the land. Until fairly recently, it was common for a family to have lived in the same town, perhaps even in the same house, for seven or eight generations. Family stories, connecting each new generation to its heritage, were handed down over the years like heirlooms.

But there is another South Carolina as well. Today's farmers have discovered new crops to plant, and new industries flourish in the state. With better transportation and communication, rural families that were once isolated have now joined the American mainstream. A civil-rights revolution has enhanced opportunities for all South Carolinians, black and white.

While South Carolinians still honor the past, they are not condemned to repeat its errors. Enriched by their traditions, they are stepping boldly toward the promise and challenges of a new century.

Chapter 2

THE LAND

THE LAND

The public being once fully persuaded of the fertility
of Carolina . . . will go to end their days in [this],
one of the most delightful countries in the universe.
—Jean Pierre Purry, a Swiss promoter who came to the
South Carolina region in the 1720s

GEOGRAPHY

On a map, South Carolina resembles a rough triangle balanced precariously on its lower tip. The Atlantic coast forms the triangle's eastern leg. Its western side is formed by the Savannah River, which divides South Carolina and Georgia. The longest side of the triangle is the boundary with North Carolina to the north.

South Carolina spreads over 31,113 square miles (80,583 square kilometers) on America's South Atlantic Coast. The state's greatest distances are 218 miles (351 kilometers) from north to south and 275 miles (443 kilometers) from east to west. South Carolina is relatively small in area, ranking fortieth among the states.

Despite its small size, South Carolina has sharp regional differences, created in part by variations in the land. Geographically, the state is divided into three regions: the Atlantic Coastal Plain, which hugs the seacoast; the Blue Ridge Mountains, which rise in the northwest corner of the state; and the Piedmont, which lies between the mountains and the coastal plain.

Lake Jocassee in the Blue Ridge Mountains

South Carolinians call the coastal plain the "Low Country," while they term the higher land of the Piedmont and the mountains the "Up Country." When engaging in small talk, natives of the state will say, "I've got an aunt living in the Up Country," or "I grew up in the Low Country, but now I live here." The terms *Up Country* and *Low Country* signify more than just a geographic division. The two land regions traditionally have harbored ways of life so different from one another that many years ago, the people of the Up Country and the Low Country almost went to war.

The Atlantic Coastal Plain spreads over the eastern two-thirds of the state. Thousands of years ago, the ocean covered the coastal plain. Today, the area near the coast is a low-lying region of swamps, marshes, and lazily flowing rivers. Farther inland on the coastal plain is a section of pine-forested land known as the Pine Barrens. At the western edge of the coastal plain is a strip of land

Above: Fall Creek Falls on Lake Keowee
in the Blue Ridge
Right: Hayrolls in the Piedmont region

called the Sand Hills. Some of the hills in this region rise 600 feet (183 meters). The capital city of Columbia lies in the Sand Hills area.

Between the coastal plain and the high ground of the Piedmont runs a narrow ledge called the Fall Line. This Fall Line extends along the East Coast of the nation from New Jersey to Georgia. As rivers tumble over this ledge to the lowlands, they churn into rapids and waterfalls. The Fall Line marks the farthest point inland where river-going ships can travel.

The Up Country begins at the Piedmont, part of a long band of gentle hills that stretches from New York to Alabama. In South Carolina, the elevation of the Piedmont region ranges from 400 to 1,200 feet (122 to 366 meters) above sea level. Rivers run swiftly across the Piedmont as the water hurries toward the Fall Line.

Above: Camping in the Blue Ridge Mountains

Many years ago, people used the surging waters to drive machinery. For that reason, South Carolina's first factories developed on the Piedmont.

The Blue Ridge Mountains cover about 500 square miles (1,295 square kilometers) in the northwest corner of the state. South Carolina's highest point, Sassafras Mountain (3,560 feet/1,085 meters), rises in the Blue Ridge. The Blue Ridge Mountains, part of the mighty Appalachian chain, are so named because their peaks radiate a soft, almost mystic blue tone when seen from a distance.

THE COAST

South Carolina's Atlantic coastline runs for some 187 miles (301 kilometers). However, if one includes all the bays, inlets,

Shorebirds at sunset on Edisto Island off the southern coast of South Carolina

islands, and peninsulas along the coast, the state can claim nearly 3,000 miles (4,828 kilometers) of waterfront. The South Carolina coast is famed as a delightful, year-round vacationland.

Along the northern third of the coast lies a strip of almost unbroken beaches often referred to as the Grand Strand. Popular resorts such as Myrtle Beach are a highlight of the northern seacoast. From the city of Georgetown to the Georgia border, the coast becomes a tangle of sandy islands and fingerlike peninsulas. So intertwined are the land and the waters on the southern portion of the state's seacoast that some children ride school boats instead of school buses to their morning classes. Some of the principal features of the southern coast are Folly Island, Kiawah Island, St. Helena Island, Hunting Island, Parris Island (which houses a Marine Corps training base), and Hilton Head Island.

South Carolina's waterways include tidal rivers that cut inland along the marshy coastal areas (left) and such picturesque interior rivers as the Congaree (right).

RIVERS AND LAKES

South Carolina has many tiny ponds, but no large natural lakes. The large lakes that exist today were created by dams built to generate electricity or to irrigate fields. The state's largest inland body of water, Lake Marion, was created in 1942 when the Santee Dam was completed. Other important man-made lakes include Lake Moultrie, Lake Murray, Lake Greenwood, Wateree Lake, and Hartwell Lake.

South Carolina is a spiderweb of rivers. Many of the rivers have Indian names given to them centuries ago by the region's earliest inhabitants. All of South Carolina's major rivers flow in a southeasterly direction from the Up Country toward the ocean. The largest of these rivers is the Santee, which drains about 40 percent of the state's water. The Santee is formed by the confluence of the Wateree and the Congaree rivers. In turn, the Congaree is the result of a merger between the Saluda and the Broad rivers. The Savannah River forms South Carolina's border with Georgia. The Pee Dee is another large river. Small rivers include the Combahee, Edisto, Ashley, Cooper, and Black.

PLANT AND ANIMAL LIFE

Hundreds of years ago, lush forests covered almost all of what is today South Carolina. So plentiful were the trees that builders in the eighteenth century threw away the outer "sap wood" of the pine logs and used only the "hearts" to make beams for houses. Building with the "hearts of pine" was a wasteful method, but the resulting beams were nearly as durable as steel and account for the magnificent, two-hundred-year-old mansions that still stand in Charleston and other historic towns.

Today, two-thirds of the state is still covered with forest. South Carolina has four large national forest areas, four state forests, and forty-seven state parks, many of which are forested. Oaks, hickories, red maples, and cypresses grow on the coastal plain. Dogwoods, oaks, and hickories are common in the Piedmont region. Groves of hemlocks stand in the Blue Ridge Mountain area. Pines of various kinds grow in all three regions. The palmetto, which grows near the coast, is the state tree. In fact, South Carolina's long-standing nickname is the Palmetto State.

In the spring, South Carolina becomes a riot of wildflowers. Common wildflowers include azaleas, goldenrod, jessamine, lilies, violets, and black-eyed Susans. A plant unique to North Carolina and South Carolina is the Venus's-flytrap, which lures flying insects onto its sticky, sweet-tasting leaves. Closing its leaves like a trap, it devours its prey. Wild fruits such as blueberries,

Lush cypress forests, spectacular
autumn foliage, white-tailed deer,
coastal sea turtles, and such
exotic plants as the Venus's-flytrap
are just a few of the gifts nature
has bestowed on South Carolina.

blackberries, cherries and plums can also be found in the state.

Roaming South Carolina's forests are herds of white-tailed deer. Black bears, though few in number, still survive in the state. Small animals include foxes, opossums, raccoons, and cottontail rabbits. A lucky hiker on a forest trail might spot a bobcat. In the swamps and marshes live alligators, snakes, and many kinds of frogs. Visitors to the wetlands must be aware of poisonous water moccasins and copperhead snakes. South Carolina boasts more than 360 species of birds, including such game birds as quail, ducks, and wild turkeys. The state's many man-made lakes are a fisherman's delight, with schools of bass, rockfish, and trout. Off South Carolina's coastal waters swim sharks, dolphins, giant turtles, and, on occasion, huge sperm whales.

CLIMATE

South Carolina has a pleasant, almost subtropical climate that remains mild even when most of the nation is suffering winter chills. During winter or summer, the coast is the warmest region of the state, the mountains are the coolest, and the Piedmont falls in between.

During the summer, the coastal plain can be miserably hot, with day after day of high humidity and temperatures above 90 degrees Fahrenheit (32 degrees Celsius). Right along the coast, however, fresh ocean breezes help make the summer more bearable. Winter in South Carolina, on the other hand, is a delight. The average January temperature is 51 degrees Fahrenheit (10.5 degrees Celsius) in the south and about 41 degrees Fahrenheit (5 degrees Celsius) in the Blue Ridge.

Extremes of both heat and cold sometimes occur in South Carolina. The mercury soared to an all-time high of 111 degrees

Tropical-storm clouds along the South Carolina coast

Fahrenheit (44 degrees Celsius) at Blackville and Calhoun Falls in September 1925 and at Camden in June 1954. On a day in January 1977, temperatures at Caesar's Head in the Blue Ridge plunged to an astonishing minus 20 degrees Fahrenheit (minus 29 degrees Celsius).

South Carolina usually receives a generous amount of rainfall, averaging about 45 inches (114 centimeters) a year. The rainiest part of the state is the Blue Ridge region, where rainfall exceeds 70 inches (178 centimeters) a year. During the winter, the forests of the Blue Ridge Mountains are often covered with snow. Snowfall is less common on the Piedmont, and it is rare in the coastal region.

Furious hurricanes sometimes lash the South Atlantic coast, destroying property and taking lives. One such devastating storm was Hurricane Camille, which struck in 1969 and killed more than 250 people from Louisiana to Virginia. Hurricanes are rare events, however, and most of the year South Carolina is blessed with a smiling sun and sparkling skies.

Chapter 3

THE
PEOPLE

THE PEOPLE

An old South Carolina is dying. A new South Carolina,
strong and vital and very proud, is struggling to be born.
We will not build the new South Carolina with brick and
mortar. We will build it with minds. The power of knowledge
and skills is our hope for survival in this new age.
—former South Carolina Governor Richard W. Riley

POPULATION AND POPULATION DISTRIBUTION

The 1980 census counted 3,122,814 people living in South
Carolina. This was a hefty 20.5 percent increase over the 1970
figure. By comparison, the population of the nation as a whole
grew 11.45 percent from 1970 to 1980. In terms of population,
South Carolina ranks twenty-fourth among the states.

Longtime residents complain that their state is becoming
crowded. South Carolina's population density averaged 100
people per square mile (39 people per square kilometer) in 1980.
In contrast, the state had only 44 people per square mile (17
people per square kilometer) at the beginning of the twentieth
century. Although South Carolina has been a mainly rural state
throughout most of its history, today the majority of South
Carolina residents—54 percent—live in cities and towns.

South Carolina's cities tend to be small. Only four cities have
populations of more than fifty thousand. In order of population,

Charleston is South Carolina's second-largest city.

the state's largest cities are Columbia, Charleston, North Charleston, Greenville, Spartanburg, and Rock Hill.

WHO ARE THE SOUTH CAROLINIANS?

Unlike many other American states, South Carolina has no large foreign-born communities. About ninety-nine out of a hundred of the state's residents were born in the United States, and three out of four were born in South Carolina. Most South Carolinians are the descendants of black and white settlers who arrived in the area centuries ago. In 1980, some six thousand Native Americans (American Indians) were living in South Carolina.

About 30 percent of South Carolinians are black. Of all the states, only Mississippi has a higher percentage of blacks in its population. During much of South Carolina's history, the

23

majority of the state's people were black. Although blacks live throughout the state, they are concentrated in the Low Country. Twelve of the state's forty-six counties have a black majority, and ten of those are Low Country counties. Few blacks live in the Blue Ridge region.

The vast majority of South Carolinians are Protestants. Baptists are the largest religious group, claiming 30 percent of the state's church members. Other important Christian denominations are the African Methodist Episcopalians, United Methodists, and Presbyterians. The state has a small but fast-growing Roman Catholic population. The state also has a small Jewish population. By the early 1800s, Charleston had a well-established Jewish community. In fact, Charleston is the home of the nation's oldest Reform Jewish synagogue.

With few foreign-born residents, English is the predominant language spoken in the state. South Carolina is home to about thirty-five thousand people of Hispanic origin. For generations, blacks living on the coastal islands spoke a colorful language called Gullah. The language is a complex blend of American English, King's English, and an African dialect. The Sea Islands are now much less isolated than they were in the past, and Gullah is fading from use.

POLITICS

From the 1880s until the middle of the twentieth century, the Democratic party controlled politics in South Carolina. Gradually, however, other parties have gained more influence in the state. In 1948, South Carolina Governor Strom Thurmond ran for president of the United States as the candidate of the short-lived "Dixiecrat" party, capturing the electoral votes of South Carolina

Strom Thurmond, shown here greeting supporters in 1954, was one of South Carolina's most powerful political leaders in the twentieth century.

and three other southern states. The Republican party gained an increased following in South Carolina during the 1960s and 1970s. In 1964, Thurmond, who had been a United States senator since 1954, left the Democratic party to become a Republican. That same year, in the presidential election, the state's electoral votes went to Republican candidate Barry Goldwater. South Carolina also voted for Republican candidates in the presidential elections of 1968, 1984, and 1988.

South Carolina's political leaders have been able to change with the times. Longtime politician Strom Thurmond once strongly favored racial segregation. But as blacks gained political power, Thurmond began to work with black citizens' groups and gave his support to black judges. Another powerful South Carolina senator and former governor, Ernest "Fritz" Hollings, shocked the nation in 1970 when he reported on hunger in South Carolina's rural areas. His efforts have done much to improve the quality of life for the state's most disadvantaged families.

Chapter 4
THE BEGINNINGS

THE BEGINNINGS

THE FIRST SOUTH CAROLINIANS

Human beings reached the land we now call South Carolina at least eleven thousand years ago. These first South Carolinians lived by hunting game and by gathering roots, nuts, and berries. Their carefully chipped stone spearpoints are still sometimes found on South Carolina hillsides.

By about 2000 B.C., the people of South Carolina had begun to clear plots of land and plant crops. They raised squash, beans, pumpkins, and their staple food—maize (corn). They learned to shape clay into useful jugs and pots.

When Europeans arrived in the 1500s, as many as forty-six distinct Native American groups, each belonging to one of four or five language families, lived in present-day South Carolina. Most of these groups were tiny, numbering only a few hundred members.

Along the coast, a number of small groups fished and gathered oysters and clams. Most of these coastal groups, including the Yamasees, the Cusabos, and the Coosas, belonged to the Muskhogean language family. The Catawbas, who were part of the Siouan language group, inhabited the northeastern part of present-day South Carolina.

In the Blue Ridge Mountains lived the powerful Cherokees, who belonged to the Iroquoian language group. Although the Cherokees numbered only about 22,000 people in 1650, they controlled 40,000 square miles (103,600 square kilometers) of mountain terrain sprawling over present-day North Carolina, South Carolina, Tennessee, and Georgia. They lived in stockaded villages and farmed communally owned land. The Cherokees had an advanced form of government in which decisions were made by a council of respected tribal members.

THE COMING OF THE EUROPEANS

The Native Americans traveled the rivers and coastal waters in long canoes made from cypress logs. They had never seen a ship with sails until a tall Spanish vessel anchored in Winyah Bay in 1521. The Native Americans hesitantly welcomed the pale-skinned strangers. After days of feasting, the Spaniards invited some 150 of the Native Americans (whom they mistakenly called Indians) to a party aboard their ship. But when the party was underway, the Spaniards suddenly set sail, taking their guests captive as slaves.

The Spaniards had come from Santo Domingo, one of Spain's new colonies in the Caribbean. They brought their Indian prisoners back to Lucas Vásquez de Ayllón, the Santo Domingo judge who had sponsored their expedition. Ayllón was angry that the Spaniards had taken the Indians captive, and ordered that they be returned to their homeland. However, one of the captives remained with Ayllón as his servant. Known as Francisco Chicora, this Indian was a remarkable storyteller. He told Ayllón marvelous tales about his homeland—which his people called Chicora—a land of ease and plenty that was ruled by a fabulous giant king.

Prom.Lup.

Porrus Regalis, ſiue F.S.Helenæ.

5

French Huguenots led by Jean Ribaut landed in the Port Royal area in 1562.

His curiosity whetted by Chicora's stories, Ayllón led a party of five hundred Spaniards and several African slaves back to Winyah Bay in 1526. There, near present-day Georgetown, they founded South Carolina's first European settlement, which they named San Miguel de Gualdape.

Almost as soon as the Spanish party touched shore, Francisco Chicora escaped into the forest. The Spaniards soon discovered that his stories had been exaggerations. Chicora was far from a paradise. Within months, two-thirds of the colonists were dead of hunger and disease, including Ayllón himself. Finally, the feeble survivors abandoned the village and returned to Santo Domingo.

Some forty years later, Europeans again tried to settle in South Carolina. In 1562, thirty French Huguenots, led by Jean Ribaut, established a tiny community in the Port Royal area. The

Huguenots were Protestants who had been persecuted in Catholic France for their religious beliefs. They hoped that they could find religious freedom in the New World. But their colony, too, was doomed. When their food supplies ran out, they tried to sail back to France. On shipboard they grew so desperate with starvation that they were forced to turn to cannibalism.

Despite their extensive territories in other parts of North America, neither Spain nor France had managed to gain a firm toehold in the region that is now South Carolina. England, however, laid claim to all of North America in the early 1600s and soon began establishing colonies along the eastern seaboard. In 1629, King Charles I of England gave a large tract of land to one of his favorite subjects, Sir Robert Heath. The land was to be called *Carolana* (the spelling was later changed to *Carolina*), a Latin term meaning "land of Charles." It was a huge territory that included the land of present-day North Carolina and South Carolina. Though Heath did little to develop this vast region, the king's grant opened a new era in South Carolina's history.

THE ENGLISH COLONY

In 1663, King Charles II, the son of Charles I, revoked Heath's title to the Carolina territory and granted the region to eight of his staunchest supporters. These eight men and their heirs were known as the lords proprietors.

At once, the proprietors began to recruit men and women to settle the land. In 1670, the first shiploads of English colonists—many of whom came from the English colony of Barbados in the Caribbean—landed on the South Carolina coast. The colony's governor, eighty-year-old William Sayle, selected a site at Albemarle Point, ten miles (sixteen kilometers) up the Ashley

River. The settlers planted cotton, sugarcane, and other crops to see which would grow best in the new land. They named the settlement Charles Towne after the English king.

The following year, the settlers were joined by about a hundred more Barbadians. There were already a few black slaves in Charles Towne, and the Barbadians brought several more. They also imported the idea, already thoroughly entrenched in the Caribbean colonies, that slavery was necessary for successful agriculture.

In 1680, the growing Charles Towne settlement was moved to Oyster Point between the Ashley and Cooper rivers, a spot that afforded an excellent harbor. As the years passed, the colony spread through the Tidewater region—the low, marshy land up and down the coast. The proprietors' insistence on religious freedom brought many colonists who had suffered persecution— French Huguenots, Quakers, Puritans, and Baptists.

With the help of Dr. Henry Woodward, who had lived with the Indians for four years before the colonists arrived, the settlers established a brisk trade in furs and deerskins. In addition to this ''peltry,'' as they called it, they exported grain, timber, and beef to England and the West Indies. In 1680, Dr. Woodward introduced a variety of rice from Madagascar. Rice flourished in the marshy soil along the coast and became a major export. By 1696, some colonists were paying their taxes in rice instead of cash.

Tensions soon flared between the colonists and their Indian neighbors. Many Indians, even those of friendly tribes, were taken as slaves. Other Indians were pressured into selling off their land. Terrible epidemics of smallpox, to which the Indians had no natural immunity, devastated the tribes and weakened their power to resist the European invaders. One colonial governor wrote, "[It has] pleased Almighty God to send unusual sicknesses

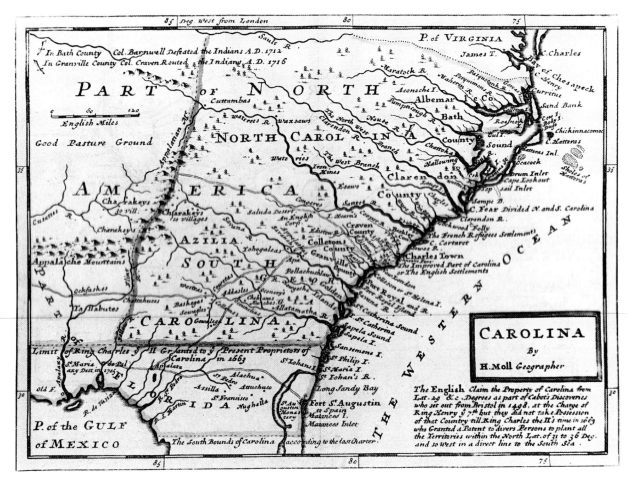

A 1739 map of the Carolinas

among them. . . . The hand of God is imminently seen in thinning the Indians to make room for the English.''

In 1715, the Yamasees tried to drive the colonists from Carolina forever. Enlisting a number of other Indian groups, the Yamasees swept up the coast, burning and pillaging as they went. Though the Indians were finally defeated at Charles Towne, the war left the colony severely weakened.

At the same time, the colonists faced another menace—pirates who marauded the coast. Buccaneers preyed upon the rich merchant ships that sailed in and out of Charles Towne Harbor. The most notorious of these pirates was Edward Teach, better known as Blackbeard. At last the colony's governor sent Colonel William Rhett to subdue the pirates. Blackbeard was killed in a bloody sea battle. Dozens of pirates were captured, and forty-nine of them were hanged on the wharf at Charles Towne.

The settlers received very little help from the lords proprietors during their struggles with the Indians and pirates. In 1719, rumors of the threat of a Spanish invasion reached the colony. When the colonists' request for soldiers and ships was denied by the colonial government, delegates from North Carolina and South Carolina petitioned the king to abolish the old proprietary form of government. (A distinction had been made between North Carolina and South Carolina since 1710, when the northern part of the colony appointed its own governor. The two regions officially became separate colonies in 1712.) Responding to the colonists' grievances, King George I declared the Carolinas to be royal provinces. In 1729, the lords proprietors formally surrendered their claim on the Carolinas, and North Carolina and South Carolina became crown colonies ruled directly by the king.

In 1730, an intelligent and skillful leader named Robert Johnson became colonial governor of South Carolina. Determined to expand the size and strength of the colony, he encouraged more Europeans to immigrate to South Carolina. Most of these new colonists settled in the wild back country (which later became known as the Up Country) inland from the coast. German-Swiss farmers cleared land at Orangeburg and along the Savannah River. Welsh immigrants farmed on the Pee Dee River. Scotch-Irish settlers (Scottish Protestants who had migrated to Ireland generations earlier) fanned out from Camden across the Piedmont. These new colonists had little in common with the slaveholding planters of the Low Country. The large rice plantations of the Low Country required a large, dependable

British pirate Edward Teach (left), better known as Blackbeard, raided ships along the Carolina coast in the early 1700s.
In the mid-1700s, settlers began establishing homesteads in the Up Country (above).

source of labor—slaves. In contrast, the Up Country settlers usually farmed only enough to support their own families, and few of them had slaves. Accordingly, very different ways of life developed in the Up Country and the Low Country.

COLONIAL LIFE

"This town makes a most beautiful appearance," wrote Josiah Quincy of Massachusetts after a visit to Charles Towne. "I can

By the mid-1700s, Charles Towne had become one of the most sophisticated cities in the thirteen British colonies.

only say that in grandeur, splendor of buildings, decorations, equipages, . . . and indeed almost everything, it far surpasses all I ever saw or ever expected to see in America.''

By the mid-1700s, the port of Charles Towne was one of the largest and most sophisticated cities in the thirteen British colonies. Its broad streets were lined with elegant mansions—the homes of wealthy rice planters and merchants. The city's elite families enjoyed an endless round of balls, concerts, theatrical performances, and hunting parties.

While a small number of planters lived in luxury, however, thousands of black slaves toiled in the fields. A few blacks managed to buy their freedom and establish themselves as farmers or skilled craftsmen. But for most black people in South Carolina, life offered little but work and degradation.

Few Up Country farmers could afford to own slaves. Often, these farmers had to struggle for the basic necessities of life. It was not uncommon for a family of ten or twelve to be crowded into a tiny, windowless log cabin, its cracks chinked with clay and moss to keep out the wind. A traveling minister, Charles Woodmason, wrote that such a family's diet might consist of "pork, cornbread, buttermilk, clabber [curdled, sour milk], and what in England is given to the hogs and dogs."

A sharp division grew between the comfortable citizens of the Low Country and their struggling Up Country neighbors. In the years ahead, this division would play a key role in South Carolina's turbulent history.

THE WAR OF INDEPENDENCE

In 1763, England signed a treaty with France ending the Seven Years' War (known in North America as the French and Indian War). The long conflict had emptied the British treasury. For revenue, England turned to her colonies in North America, passing the Stamp Act in 1765. The act required American colonists to buy official stamps whenever they purchased newspapers, legal documents, or even playing cards.

The people of Charles Towne were outraged. Mobs broke into the homes of British sympathizers, searching for stamps. When a Stamp Act Congress met in New York, three South Carolina delegates attended. One of them, Christopher Gadsden, urged the colonies to unite for greater strength: "There ought to be no New England man, no New Yorker . . . but all of us Americans."

England repealed the Stamp Act, only to replace it with a new set of taxes on glass, wine, copper, paper, tea, and many other imported items. Even after most of these taxes, too, were repealed, tension continued to mount between the colonies and the mother country.

In 1775, a secret committee met in Charles Towne and appointed thirteen members to a Council of Safety. In April, when British troops and colonial militia exchanged fire at Lexington, Massachusetts, the council prepared South Carolina for war.

The small Up Country farmers, however, did not want war with England. Import taxes hardly concerned them, and they feared that war would stir up trouble with their neighbors, the Cherokees. Many people in the Up Country became British sympathizers, or Tories. In November 1775, the Council of Safety sent five hundred militiamen to suppress Tory resistance. Though many Tory leaders were captured, pro-British feeling remained strong in the South Carolina hills. Most South Carolinians, however, aligned themselves with the patriots, or Whigs, who favored independence.

Charles Towne was the most strategic port on the South Atlantic Coast. In June 1776, British naval forces tried to take the city, but they were driven back. The following month, four South Carolina delegates to the Continental Congress in Philadelphia signed the Declaration of Independence. The ties with England were severed forever.

During the war years, South Carolina saw nearly 140 skirmishes and battles. Not all of these battles were between the Whigs and the British. So much fighting occurred between Whigs and Tories that the state was virtually wracked by a civil war.

By the spring of 1780, most South Carolinians were weary of bloodshed. In May, Charles Towne fell to the British, and the

In June 1776, when British forces intent on taking Charles Towne attacked Fort Moultrie on Sullivan's Island, Sergeant William Jasper rescued the fort's flag. Colonial forces ultimately defeated the British in this battle, and eventually, a version of this flag became the South Carolina state flag.

Southern Continental army surrendered. The British general, Henry Clinton, wrote, "I may venture to assert that there are few men in South Carolina who are not prisoners of war or in arms with us."

Yet the British still had to contend with the guerrilla tactics of Andrew "Fighting Elder" Pickens, Thomas "the Gamecock" Sumter and Francis "the Swamp Fox" Marion. These three South Carolina patriots harassed the British in the mountains, among the sand hills, and through the tidewater marshes. Yet, despite the efforts of wily guerrillas, South Carolina teetered on the brink of defeat.

Then an episode occurred that rekindled anti-British feeling throughout South Carolina. Word swept from town to town that

The guerrilla tactics of General Francis Marion, shown here crossing the Pee Dee River, earned him the nickname the "Swamp Fox."

British General Banastre Tarleton had massacred a retreating force of Continental soldiers near the town of Lancaster even though their leader had waved the white flag of surrender. Even dedicated Tories were appalled at the news.

On October 7, 1780, a ragtag force of frontiersmen from the Blue Ridge Mountains encircled British Major Patrick Ferguson's encampment on Kings Mountain, just south of the North Carolina

Colonial troops were victorious in the 1781 Battle of Cowpens.

border. Ferguson, who gave orders to his troops with blasts on a great silver whistle, was killed, along with nearly four hundred of his men. The rest were taken prisoner. The Battle of Kings Mountain was instrumental in turning the tide in favor of the Continental forces in the South.

Early in 1781, Continental troops confronted the treacherous General Tarleton at Cowpens, a gathering place for cattle on long drives to the coast. Some eleven hundred of Tarleton's men were killed or captured. In 1782, the British abandoned Charles Towne, and in 1783, the war came to an end.

Peace had come at last. Now South Carolina faced the challenge of forging an identity within a struggling new nation.

Chapter 5
UNION AND SECESSION

UNION AND SECESSION

"The Constitution, with all its imperfections, is the only thing that can rescue the states from civil discord," wrote Pierce Butler, one of South Carolina's delegates to the Constitutional Convention of 1787. Yet, through the tumultuous decades that followed, South Carolinians debated what the Constitution meant for their state.

COTTON BECOMES KING

After the Revolutionary War, tension persisted between the Up Country farmers and their Low Country neighbors. The people of the Up Country, fearing that the wealthy Low Country planters and merchants would control the state legislature, demanded a fair representation in the government. As a compromise, the legislators agreed to move the capital away from Charles Towne (whose name was changed to Charleston in 1783 because it sounded less British). In 1786, a team of surveyors laid out a new city in the center of the state, at the juncture of the Broad and Saluda rivers. Columbia, which officially became the state's capital in 1790, became one of the first planned cities in the United States.

In 1787, four South Carolina delegates attended the Constitutional Convention in Philadelphia to help draw up a code of laws for governing the new nation. Charles Pinckney of

In the early 1800s, cotton became South Carolina's leading cash crop.

Charleston is thought to have presented an early plan for the United States Constitution. Although what has been called the "Pinckney Draft" has never been found, Pinckney's ideas clearly influenced our system of representative government.

In 1793, a Connecticut engineer named Eli Whitney patented a simple machine that revolutionized agriculture in South Carolina. Whitney's cotton gin removed the seeds from the valuable cotton fiber faster than a dozen workers could do by hand. Before the invention of the cotton gin, large-scale cotton production had never been profitable. Now, within a few short years, cotton eclipsed rice and indigo as South Carolina's leading cash crop. Planters and speculators made fortunes, and cotton became king

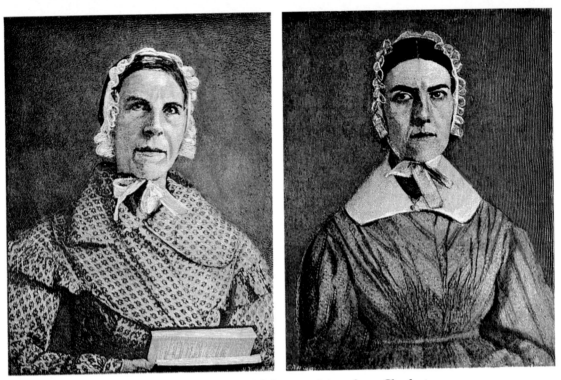

Sarah Grimké (left) and Angelina Grimké (right) were sisters from Charleston who became dedicated abolitionists.

in South Carolina. To produce cotton cheaply, the planters depended on slaves to tend and harvest their crops. South Carolina became ever more deeply enmeshed in the slave system.

In 1822, Denmark Vesey, a free black man from Charleston, tried to organize an uprising among the city's slaves. The conspiracy was discovered, and Vesey and thirty-four of his followers were hanged. News of the thwarted rebellion filled white South Carolinians with fear. How much longer could they keep the state's large black population under control?

Almost as worrisome as potential slave uprisings was the new abolition movement that was gaining strength in the northern states. By the 1830s, eloquent blacks and whites were arguing from speaker's platforms that slavery should be abolished. Some South Carolinians agreed, deeply troubled by the inhumanity of their society. Sarah and Angelina Grimké, sisters from a genteel Charleston family, became dedicated abolitionists. The Grimké sisters spoke passionately of the horrors of slavery they had witnessed. In a speech in Philadelphia, Angelina declared, "I have seen it! . . . I grew up under its wing! I witnessed for many years

. . . [It is] absolutely necessary to keep the blacks in their present condition."

THE NULLIFICATION CRISIS

In the late 1820s and early 1830s, another issue wracked South Carolina and threatened to break the state's ties to the federal government. In 1828, to the dismay of planters and merchants, Congress passed a bill that raised the tariffs (taxes) imposed on goods imported from foreign countries. This so-called "Tariff of Abominations" benefited northern industry, because it made foreign goods more expensive and thus encouraged Americans to buy goods made in the United States. Southern cotton growers, however, depended on trade with Europe. They feared that imposing high tariffs on European goods would cause the Europeans to retaliate by refusing to buy American cotton. The planters found a champion in Vice-President John C. Calhoun, a South Carolina native. Calhoun was an ardent defender of states' rights—the idea that each state should be free to direct its internal affairs without federal interference. After the 1828 tariff act was

Vice-President John C. Calhoun, the most famous South Carolina-born politician of the nineteenth century, was an ardent defender of states' rights.

passed, Calhoun wrote a resolution that became known as the South Carolina Exposition. This resolution, which was quickly approved by the South Carolina legislature, held that a state could declare null and void any act of Congress it considered unconstitutional. The "nullifiers" argued that since it was the states who had created the federal government, they should have the right to determine when they felt Congress had exceeded its powers. When Congress passed yet another tariff act in 1832, South Carolinians responded by passing the Ordinance of Nullification, which nullified the tariff acts of 1828 and 1832.

Calhoun's fiercest opponent was a fellow South Carolinian, President Andrew Jackson. When South Carolina threatened to leave the Union, or secede, rather than pay the tariffs, Jackson prepared to send federal troops to his home state. However, a compromise was finally reached. Congress lowered the tariffs, the Ordinance of Nullification was repealed, and the crisis passed.

Triumphantly, Jackson wrote, "Thus died nullification and the doctrines of secession, never more to be heard of."

President Jackson could not have been further from the truth.

A HOUSE DIVIDED

...sion of slavery into the nation's western territories. If the abolitionists halted the spread of slavery, white South Carolinians reasoned, they might also forbid it in states where it already existed.

In 1850, Kentucky Senator Henry Clay proposed a compromise that would allow slavery in some, but not all, of the western territories. Most of the southern states accepted the Compromise of 1850, but South Carolina saw any restriction of slavery as a threat. As the Winyah *Observer* put it, "To us the Union as it is is a curse and not a blessing. It is . . . an engine of oppression."

Created in 1856, the Republican party was the voice of the antislavery movement. In a speech at the Illinois State Republican Convention two years later, a tall, homely young lawyer named Abraham Lincoln proclaimed, "A house divided against itself cannot stand. I believe this government cannot endure permanently half slave and half free." Most white South Carolinians felt that Lincoln embodied the worst of the abolitionist North. They were outraged when he ran for president of the United States in 1860. They feared that if Lincoln were elected, he would free all the slaves in the South.

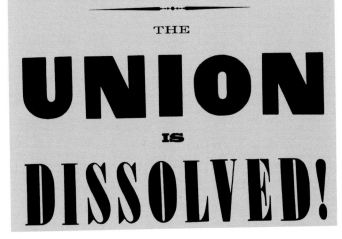

The day after
South Carolina seceded
from the Union, the
Charleston Mercury
shouted this confident
headline.

On November 6, 1860, Lincoln was elected sixteenth president of the United States. Even before he could be sworn into office, the South Carolina legislature called a state convention to plan for secession. Convinced that the rest of the slaveholding states would follow its example, South Carolina passed the Ordinance of Secession on December 20. The next day, a Charleston headline shouted the news, "UNION IS DISSOLVED."

THE WAR BETWEEN THE STATES

During the winter of 1861, ten more slaveholding states seceded. Together they formed the Confederate States of America.

The Civil War began on April 12, 1861, when Confederate forces attacked Fort Sumter in Charleston Harbor.

In the words of Charleston poet Henry Timrod, the Confederacy would stand as "a nation among nations."

In his inaugural address, President Lincoln told the Confederacy, "You have no oath sworn in heaven to destroy the government, while I have the most solemn one to preserve, protect, and defend it." In both the North and the South, people waited with fear and excitement to see what would happen. The United States could not let the South go without a struggle. From the moment South Carolina seceded, civil war was inevitable.

Near the mouth of Charleston Harbor stood Fort Sumter, one of a handful of United States forts within the boundaries of the Confederacy. On April 11, 1861, Confederate officers met with United States Major Robert Anderson, the fort's commander, and demanded his immediate surrender. Anderson refused.

Just before dawn on April 12, a Confederate shell flew in a long arc across the harbor and burst over Fort Sumter. All around the

Proud Confederate militiamen pose beside captured guns on the parade ground of Fort Sumter.

harbor, Confederate artillery opened fire. According to one eyewitness, "Showers of balls . . . and shells . . . poured into the fort in one incessant stream, causing great flakes of mortar to fall in all directions. When the immense mortar shells . . . buried themselves in the parade ground, their explosion shook the fort like an earthquake." After thirty-four hours, Anderson lowered the Stars and Stripes, and Fort Sumter surrendered. The first battle may have been over—but the war had only begun.

In South Carolina, thousands of young men volunteered to serve in the Confederate army. Townspeople cheered and bands played as the soldiers marched out in their new gray uniforms. They felt certain that the Yankees would soon turn tail, and the boys in gray would come home in triumph.

But the war soon proved to be a serious business. In November 1861, Union troops launched a massive assault on the South Carolina coast. After the Yankees seized Port Royal and Hilton

This 1863 drawing shows Charlestonians running for cover as a Union shell bursts in the street.

Head, even the people of Charleston wondered if they were safe.

Although the city of Charleston did not fall into Union hands, the United States Navy blockaded Charleston Harbor. South Carolina's supplies of food and medicine ran dangerously low. The people faced other hardships as well. Since most of the men were away at war, the women had to carry out the farmwork in addition to their other household duties. Many women volunteered as nurses, tending the wounded in makeshift hospitals under appalling conditions at the front.

As the war dragged on, Confederate losses grew heavier. Morale began to crumble. Hundreds of soldiers deserted, many taking refuge in the Blue Ridge Mountains. One gang of deserters took over an island in the Broad River and held it as a fortified camp. Yet the embattled Confederacy fought on, struggling for survival against hunger, disease, and mounting casualties.

In the winter of 1864-65, Union General William T. Sherman dealt the Confederacy its death blow. After capturing Atlanta, Sherman's army marched across Georgia to the sea, cutting a path of destruction as it went. When Sherman reached Savannah, he turned north into South Carolina.

It is said that General Sherman coined the phrase "War is hell." He waged a brutal brand of warfare never before seen in America—a war not against enemy armies, but against civilians. In South Carolina, Sherman's army destroyed crops, slaughtered livestock, and burned farmhouses. When they reached Columbia, Sherman's men went on a drunken rampage. Before officers could get their men under control, they had looted hundreds of homes and set fire to the city, where thousands of refugees had taken shelter.

Surveying the ruins, one Ohio congressman called the burning of Columbia "the most monstrous barbarity of the barbarous march." But Sherman later wrote, "Though I never ordered it and

Union troops
under the command of
General William T.
Sherman left Columbia

never wished it, I have never shed any tears over the event, because I believe that it hastened what we all fought for — the end of the war." On April 9, 1865, Confederate commander Robert E. Lee surrendered at Appomattox Court House, Virginia.

On April 14, almost precisely four years after the first shots of the war were fired, Major Robert Anderson returned to raise the Stars and Stripes over Fort Sumter. At the ceremony, the Reverend Henry Ward Beecher offered a message of hope for the future:

> We raise our fathers' banner . . . that it may cast out the devil of discord; that it may restore lawful government and a prosperity purer and more enduring than that which it protected before; that it may . . . purify our principles, ennoble our national ambitions, and make this people great and strong . . . for the peace of the world.

Just hours after Beecher's hopeful words rang out, President Abraham Lincoln lay dying, the victim of an assassin's bullet.

Most former slaves who stayed in the South after the war became tenant farmers.

THE RECONSTRUCTION ERA

Some historians believe that, if he had lived, President Lincoln would have developed a just and effective program for rebuilding the South and bringing it back into the Union. As it was, the postwar years, known as the era of Reconstruction, have sometimes been called the "rule of the robbers."

The war left South Carolina in ruins. A quarter of the young men who served in the Confederate army had died. Many who returned home found their fields overgrown and their livestock stolen or slaughtered. The large plantations were suddenly without the slave labor that had sustained them for nearly two hundred years.

With the close of the war, slavery was abolished forever. Many former slaves, known as freedmen, wandered from town to town, rejoicing in the knowledge that no master could tell them when to

come and go. But few freedmen had land or steady work. Freedom, so long awaited, brought a new set of problems.

The Fourteenth Amendment to the United States Constitution prohibited the states from denying a person civil rights on the basis of race. In 1867, federal troops occupied South Carolina and the other southern states to oversee the registration of black voters. The following year, seventy-six blacks and forty-eight whites, many of them from the North, held a convention to draw up a new state constitution, and South Carolina was accepted back into the Union. The new constitution abolished debtors' prisons, eliminated the rule that people running for office must be property holders, and called for the state to build a system of public schools. The constitution of 1868 seemed to pave the way to a brighter future for all South Carolinians—rich and poor, black and white.

With the new constitution in force, black South Carolinians not only voted, but held public office throughout the state. White

South Carolinians, feeling their power base crumbling, were alarmed. Journalist James S. Pike lamented in 1873, "Seven years ago, these [black] men were raising cotton and corn under the whip of the overseer. Today they are raising points of order and questions of privilege."

Some of the state's Reconstruction-era officials, such as Secretary of State Francis L. Cardozo, were honest, hardworking men who were deeply concerned for their constituents. However, many officials, both black and white, were highly corrupt. Most white South Carolinians loathed the northern Republicans, or "carpetbaggers," who flocked south after the war. Perhaps even more deeply resented were the "scalawags," southern whites who supported the Republicans. Buying votes for themselves and manipulating other public officials, the carpetbaggers and scalawags exploited the instability of the defeated Confederacy.

In South Carolina, many carpetbaggers grew rich and powerful, ignoring the desperate needs of their adopted state. New schools and roads remained dreams as Republican officials siphoned off public funds to purchase elegant furniture and china, and dined on the most expensive delicacies money could buy. As one carpetbagger described the atmosphere: "Even breathing it made one feel like going out and picking a pocket."

In an attempt to bring back the old order, some white South Carolinians turned to the newly formed Ku Klux Klan, a secret organization that spread rapidly across the South. On dark nights, white-robed, hooded Klansmen raided the homes of carpetbaggers and what they termed "uppity" blacks. The Klan terrorized and murdered those it defined as enemies of white supremacy. In 1871, after an explosion of Klan-triggered violence, President Ulysses S. Grant placed nine Up Country counties under martial law.

During the gubernatorial election of 1876, Governor Daniel Chamberlain, a Republican from Massachusetts, was challenged by a Confederate Civil War hero, General Wade Hampton. When the votes were counted, both candidates claimed victory. For four days, Hampton and Chamberlain sat in the same room in the capitol, each trying to conduct the state's business, while crowds outside cheered, booed, and threatened to riot. Even after the state supreme court awarded the election to Hampton, Chamberlain refused to back down. For months, South Carolina operated under a dual government. Hampton had the overwhelming support of the old planter aristocracy, but federal troops were on hand to defend Chamberlain and the Republicans.

In the spring of 1877, President Rutherford B. Hayes brought the conflict to an end by withdrawing all federal troops from South Carolina. At last, Chamberlain gave up the struggle, and Wade Hampton became South Carolina's first Democratic governor since the war. The era of Reconstruction—its ideals and its corruption—had come to an end.

Chapter 6

INTO THE TWENTIETH CENTURY

_____ food, the exposition featured displays of fine cotton fabrics and splendid fruits and vegetables. In industry and agriculture, South Carolina had made dramatic progress since the Civil War, and it wanted the world to see its achievements.

Real gains had been made, yet South Carolinians still faced a long struggle toward economic prosperity and social justice in the twentieth century.

THE OLD AND THE NEW

To the planter aristocracy, General Wade Hampton embodied the best of the Old South. He had fought nobly for the Confederacy, and the planters believed that as governor of South Carolina, he would restore the state to its former glory.

But the Old South they yearned for was not revived. For one thing, blacks now had the right to vote, and some served in the state legislature. To the dismay of many white South Carolinians, Hampton said he was "willing to trust [the blacks], as they ask only the rights guaranteed to them by the Constitution of the United States and of our own state."

Also, as the years passed, the farmers of the Up Country

demanded a greater voice in the government. In 1885, Bennettsville farmers cheered Benjamin Tillman, an outspoken young man from Edgefield County, when he delivered a fiery speech about the evils of the government and the business community.

Tillman's reputation grew as he crossed and recrossed the state, championing the cause of South Carolina's small farmers. He argued that the state should open an agricultural college that would teach the most up-to-date farming methods. At every opportunity, he criticized the Low Country planters, the merchants, and the owners of the railroad companies that charged exorbitant rates for shipping farm produce. To an audience in Charleston, he declared, "You are the most self-idolatrous people in the world. I want to tell you that the sun doesn't rise and set in Charleston."

Ben Tillman, known as "Pitchfork Ben" because he once said he would like to stab the president of the United States with a pitchfork, claimed to be a man of the people. Yet, while he defended South Carolina's poor white farmers, he thwarted improvements for the state's blacks. When he was elected governor in 1890, he set out to disenfranchise black South Carolinians. Since about 78 percent of the state's blacks could not read or write, Tillman and his followers established a literacy requirement for voter registration. They were careful to provide loopholes, however, that allowed many illiterate whites to vote. In 1895, the Tillmanites wrote a new state constitution that placed even tighter restrictions on black voters. According to the state's Democratic committee, the aim of the new document was "to obviate all future danger and fortify Anglo-Saxon Civilization."

By the turn of the century, the strict separation of blacks and whites was the law of the land throughout the South. A series of

A cartoonist's conception of
fiery South Carolina politician
"Pitchfork Ben" Tillman

"Jim Crow" laws enforced the time-honored custom of
segregation. These laws required blacks to use separate waiting
rooms, railroad cars, and drinking fountains.

State spending on black schools dwindled to a trickle. Lynching
black suspects was tacitly approved as a form of justice. By 1900,
nearly all of the gains blacks had made after the Civil War had
eroded away.

HARD TIMES EVERYWHERE

With Ben Tillman's support, Clemson College, an agricultural school, opened in 1893 to teach the newest, most-effective techniques of crop management. However, the college helped only a lucky few. Economic hardships had caused many once-wealthy planters to sell off parcels of land year by year. In 1860, the average plantation had covered 347 acres (140 hectares). Thirty years later, the average plantation size had shrunk to only 90 acres (36 hectares). Worse still, thousands of South Carolina farmers had no land of their own, and instead worked on another's land as tenant farmers, or sharecroppers.

Under the sharecropping system, the tenant farmer turned over a share of his crop to the landowner. The other part of the crop was his to sell. But between one harvest and the next, the tenant farmer's family needed food and clothing. The tenant farmer had to purchase these items on credit at the country store. When he sold his cotton and corn, most of his profit went to pay off his debts.

Debt bound the sharecroppers to the land they worked. For white sharecroppers, however, there was a ray of hope. They could leave the land for work in the cotton mills.

A SHIFT TOWARD INDUSTRY

Throughout its history, South Carolina had relied on agriculture—first rice, then cotton—to be the mainstay of its economy. In the 1840s, an inventive South Carolinian named William Gregg urged the state to develop industry as well. In 1845, Gregg established the manufacturing village of Graniteville in the Horse Creek Valley near Aiken. The village was complete

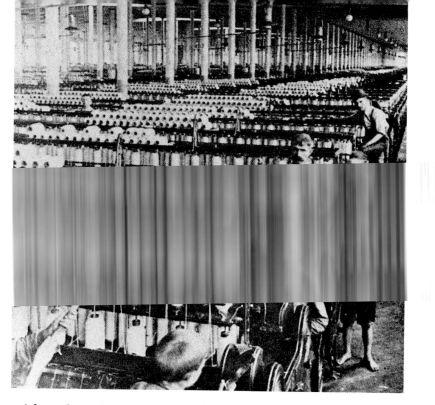

with a church, a school, and homes for the workers. About three hundred people worked in Gregg's mill, weaving raw cotton fiber into fabric.

Few mills appeared before the Civil War. But many factories opened in the 1870s and 1880s, using the mill at Graniteville as their model. The swiftly flowing rivers of South Carolina's Piedmont region proved an excellent source of power. By 1905, thirty-seven thousand men, women, and children worked in the cotton mill belt across Anderson, Greenville, and Spartanburg counties.

Most of these textile factories refused to hire workers who were black. Even for white workers, the wages were pitifully low — averaging 72 cents a day for adults, and only 25 cents a day for children. To meet their most basic needs, whole families worked ten-hour days, six days a week. Instead of attending school, children as young as eight or nine spent their days tying broken strands of yarn or replacing full bobbins with empty ones.

The mill towns were isolated communities, and the workers depended on company-owned stores for their food and clothing — much as they had once depended on the country stores. Like the sharecroppers, they were often trapped by debt, submerged at the bottom of the economic heap. Though they were better off than the sharecroppers, the mill workers still led a difficult life. As the refrain of an old song says: "It's a hard time, cotton mill girls, It's a hard time everywhere!"

INTO THE MAINSTREAM

As the twentieth century dawned, four-fifths of all South Carolinians lived on farms or in small towns. These rural people had little contact with the world outside their immediate communities. Most country roads were unpaved. Illiteracy was high among blacks and poor whites. By 1910, South Carolina had only thirteen high schools.

Few rural homes had indoor toilets or running water. Hospitals were widely scattered and poorly staffed. Smallpox, typhoid, and malaria were common. Another serious health problem was pellagra, a debilitating condition caused by poor nutrition.

Then, very slowly, the quality of life began to improve. In 1905, a state law required vaccination against smallpox. Grants from the Rockefeller Foundation helped establish the state's first county boards of health in 1915. In 1917, after a long and bitter struggle, the practice of child labor in the textile mills was abolished. During the 1920s, new highways were built throughout the state.

Farm prices soared when, in 1917, the United States entered World War I. Thousands of recruits trained at Camp Jackson near Columbia, Camp Sevier at Greenville, and Camp Wadsworth outside Spartanburg. Many South Carolinians, especially rural

blacks, left their home state to seek jobs in northern factories. The black exodus continued after the war. In 1922, for the first time in about a hundred years, whites outnumbered blacks in South Carolina.

The wartime boom was short-lived. In the 1920s, South Carolina had a new inhabitant—a small, grayish beetle with a long snout—that had been steadily migrating north from Mexico since the 1890s. This newcomer was called the boll weevil.

The boll weevil lays its eggs in the fruit, or boll, of the cotton plant. Inside the boll, the larvae devour the seeds and cotton fiber. They then emerge as adults to lay more eggs and begin the cycle over again. In 1921, boll weevils destroyed half of South Carolina's cotton crop.

The boll weevil taught South Carolina farmers that they could no longer depend on cotton alone, but instead must diversify their crops. Almost 50 percent of South Carolina's farmland was planted in cotton in 1919. By 1938, this figure had dropped to a

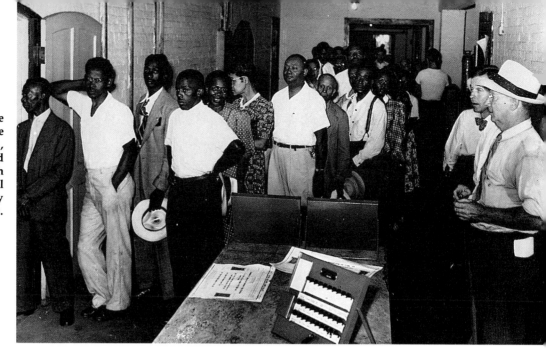

In 1948, for the first time since Reconstruction, blacks were allowed to vote in South Carolina's crucial Democratic primary elections.

mere 10 percent. During the 1920s and 1930s, farmers experimented with such crops as grapes, peaches, asparagus, and soybeans.

In the 1930s, the United States plunged into a devastating economic depression. South Carolina was hit especially hard. Mills closed and farm prices tumbled. Recovery programs under President Franklin D. Roosevelt's New Deal put many South Carolinians back to work building roads, bridges, and schools. Federal programs also helped to restore millions of acres of land that had been depleted by excessive cotton farming.

National prosperity returned in 1940, as the country readied itself for World War II. During the war, Charleston emerged as a military center with the establishment of a key naval base. The war inspired a fresh wave of South Carolinians to leave the farms and textile mills in search of work in the whirring factories of the northern cities.

More and more South Carolinians were being touched by new experiences and ideas. Yet few of them could have envisioned the vast changes that would sweep their state in the decades to come.

MEETING THE CHALLENGES

Military-related activities continued in the Charleston area even

colleagues once remarked, "You put anything else down there in your district, Mendel, and it's gonna sink."

Politics in South Carolina were completely controlled by the Democratic party during this time. Blacks were not eligible to vote in the crucial Democratic primary elections. In 1948, a courageous federal district judge from Charleston, J. Waites Waring, ruled that these "white primaries" were unconstitutional. In his decision, Waring wrote, "South Carolina is now the only state which conducts a primary election solely for whites. It is time for South Carolina to rejoin the Union."

A 1954 decision by the United States Supreme Court further challenged the laws and customs that made blacks second-class citizens in most southern states. In the case *Brown vs. Topeka* (Kansas) *Board of Education*, the court ruled that maintaining separate public schools for blacks and whites was unconstitutional. The court ordered that public schools be desegregated to allow black and white children to be educated together.

Rather than have their children attend integrated schools, many white South Carolinians preferred to keep them out of school altogether. In 1955, the South Carolina legislature repealed the state's compulsory school-attendance law.

In Washington, D.C., South Carolina Senator Strom Thurmond fought relentlessly against civil-rights legislation. In one speech, he declared, "There are not enough troops in the army to force southern people to admit the Negro into our theaters, swimming pools, and homes."

Gradually, however, led by some key figures in the government and business communities, hard-line segregationists began to yield. In fact, desegregation proceeded more smoothly and peacefully in South Carolina than in many other southern states. In 1963, Governor Ernest "Fritz" Hollings welcomed Harvey Gantt, the first black student ever to register at Clemson University. Compulsory education in South Carolina was reinstated in 1967. Statewide desegregation of the schools was finally underway by 1970. Though many white South Carolinians had wanted to avoid this moment, it passed with few incidents of violent protest.

Even before the schools were desegregated, the Colored Only and Whites Only signs disappeared from waiting rooms, lunch counters, and public fountains. Blacks no longer had to ride at the back of the bus. By the early 1970s, about one of every five textile workers was black.

Underlying the changes for blacks in South Carolina was the federal Voting Rights Act of 1965, which struck down state laws that disenfranchised black voters. For the first time since Reconstruction, black citizens had a direct voice in their government. Blacks comprised 30 percent of South Carolina's population, and they loomed as a powerful political force. Even Strom Thurmond, once the outspoken foe of civil rights, began to court his black constituents during the 1970s and 1980s. By 1982, blacks held 22 of the 124 seats in the General Assembly.

South Carolina's economic profile changed radically in the

postwar decades. Between 1939 and 1972, the number of factories in the state almost tripled. Textile manufacturing expanded as

South Carolinians in the years after World War II. Scattered one-room schoolhouses consolidated to form regional elementary and secondary schools that could offer students a broader education than ever before. Though life in the country became more comfortable, South Carolinians followed the growing national trend of abandoning the family farm and taking jobs in town.

By the 1980s, South Carolinians had become increasingly concerned with the quality of their natural environment. When the Savannah River Plant began operating near Aiken in 1953, it was hailed as a miracle of modern technology. The plant was designed to manufacture materials vital to the production of nuclear weapons, especially radioactive tritium. In the 1980s, however, public concern about the safety of the Savannah River Plant mounted. Residents of Aiken and neighboring communities were stunned when three of its four reactors were shut down for safety violations in the summer of 1988.

As South Carolina works to resolve its long-standing problems, it gains momentum on its journey into a challenging new century. In 1972, Ernest Hollings declared, "We of today must realize the lesson of one hundred years ago, and move on for the good of South Carolina and the United States."

Chapter 7

GOVERNMENT AND THE ECONOMY

Although South Carolina's state constitution was adopted in 1895, it has been amended more than 350 times. Like the federal government, South Carolina's government is divided into three branches. The legislative branch makes the laws, the judicial branch interprets the laws, and the executive branch ensures that the laws are enforced.

South Carolina's legislature, called the General Assembly, consists of two houses. In the upper house, or senate, 46 members are elected to four-year terms. In the lower house, or house of representatives, 124 members serve two-year terms. The legislature meets every year to vote on new bills.

The General Assembly elects five justices to serve ten-year terms on the South Carolina Supreme Court. The supreme court is the highest court within the state's judicial system. Below the supreme court are several circuit courts and general-sessions courts that handle criminal and civil cases. Each of South Carolina's forty-six counties has a county court, and many towns have magistrate's courts.

Elected officials in the executive branch of the state government include the superintendent of education, state treasurer, secretary of state, commissioner of agriculture, attorney general, and

Cadets at The Citadel, The Military College of South Carolina

lieutenant governor. The governor, or chief executive, is elected to a four-year term and may serve two terms in a row. Many South Carolina governors, including Benjamin Tillman, Strom Thurmond, and Ernest Hollings, later moved on to long careers in the United States Senate.

About 40 percent of South Carolina's revenue comes from federal grants and programs. Individual income tax and sales taxes generate the remaining state funds. The largest item in South Carolina's annual budget is education.

EDUCATION

In 1710, South Carolina's colonial legislature established a system of "free schools." White children from poor families attended free of charge, while families with means paid tuition. What was probably the nation's first school for young blacks was established in Charleston by Reverend Alexander Garden in 1743.

Only the larger cities could afford to establish free schools for whites, and the education of blacks was discouraged during the state's early history. Education for all finally became a reality in the twentieth century. Today, all South C[illegible]

[illegible] students at [illegible] campus in Columbia. The Medical University of South Carolina in Charleston trains future physicians. Also near Charleston is The Military College of South Carolina, known as The Citadel. The Citadel is one of only three state-sponsored military colleges in the nation.

With an enrollment of about five thousand, Bob Jones University at Greenville is the largest fundamentalist college in the country. It is not affiliated with any specific religious group, but its curriculum is built around the study of the Bible. Other privately funded colleges in the state include Converse College and Wofford College in Spartanburg, Coker College in Hartsville, Erskine College in Due West, Furman University in Greenville, and Newberry College in Newberry.

TRANSPORTATION

Cars and trucks roll over nearly 63,000 miles (101,386 kilometers) of roads to every corner of South Carolina. The state is also crisscrossed by 3,000 miles (4,828 kilometers) of railroad track. Most trains operating in the state carry only freight, but passenger trains still serve five cities.

Charleston is one of South Carolina's three seaports.

South Carolina has three seaports: Charleston, Georgetown, and Port Royal. The Atlantic Intracoastal Waterway provides a sheltered passage for vessels that wish to avoid the islands and sandbars along the coast. South Carolina has about seventy-five public airfields. The state's largest airports are located in Columbia and Charleston.

COMMUNICATION

Some ninety-five newspapers are published regularly in South Carolina. Fifteen of these are dailies. Leading papers in the state include the *News and Courier* of Charleston, the *State* of Columbia, the *Anderson Independent-Mail,* and the *Spartanburg Herald-Journal.*

Radio came to South Carolina in 1930, when WSPA went on the air in Spartanburg. South Carolina has 165 AM and FM stations

South Carolina is a leading producer of tobacco (left) and peaches (right).

today. The state's first television station, WCOS-TV of Columbia, began broadcasting in 1953. The South Carolina Educational Television network, established in 1958, is considered one of the best educational networks in the United States. Currently, South Carolina has about 30 television stations.

AGRICULTURE

Once the backbone of South Carolina's economy, farming now accounts for only 1 percent of the gross state product, or GSP (the total value of all goods and services produced in the state each year). Though this figure of 1 percent sounds small, farming is still big business in the Palmetto State. About 6 million acres (2.4 million hectares) of land are under cultivation. Cotton is still grown in Lee and Marlboro counties, but it is no longer king in South Carolina. Today the state's leading crop is tobacco, followed by soybeans and corn. South Carolina raises more peaches than any other state except California. Other crops include apples, hay, oats, peanuts, pecans, potatoes, tomatoes, and watermelons.

Poultry farms in South Carolina produce eggs, broiler chickens, and turkeys. South Carolina farmers also raise hogs, dairy cattle, and beef cattle.

MANUFACTURING

Manufacturing accounts for 28 percent of South Carolina's GSP. Only North Carolina ranks higher in the production of textiles. The old-fashioned mills where workers toiled over clattering machinery amid choking clouds of cotton lint have long since disappeared. Today's highly mechanized factories turn out fabrics of cotton, silk, and wool, as well as polyesters, acrylics, and nylons. Textile manufacturing is concentrated in the Piedmont, especially around Spartanburg, Greenville, and Anderson. Other factories in the Piedmont assemble machinery used in the textile industry. Many factories in the state turn natural and synthetic fabrics into finished clothing.

The chemical industry is a relative newcomer to South Carolina. Plants in Charleston, Columbia, and Greenville make a variety of fertilizers. The Savannah River Plant, operated by the federal government, produces radioactive materials used in the defense and aerospace industries.

SERVICE INDUSTRIES

Nearly two-thirds of South Carolina's GSP is contributed by service industries. Instead of producing saleable goods, workers in the service industries provide services to groups or individuals. The largest employers in this category are the state and federal

Textile manufacturing is South Carolina's leading industry.

governments. The military, with air force and naval bases at Charleston, the army base of Fort Jackson at Columbia, and the Marine Corps Recruiting Depot at Parris Island, provides jobs for thousands of South Carolinians. Wholesale and retail trade are also important service industries. Cargo ships from all over the world load and unload at Charleston's docks. Greenville is a major center of textile trade.

Tourism creates jobs for South Carolinians in state parks, national forests, restaurants, and hotels. The glittering beach resorts at Hilton Head Island and along the Grand Strand bring billions of dollars into the state each year. Lured by the romance of the Old South and the state's entrancing natural beauty, visitors are a boon to South Carolina's economy.

Chapter 8
ARTS AND LEISURE

ARTS AND LEISURE

The forces that shaped South Carolina's history also molded much of its art, literature, and music. The fine arts in the Palmetto State reflect the diverse backgrounds and perspectives of its people. In the performing arts and in the field of athletics, South Carolinians have excelled and made enduring contributions.

LITERATURE

Born in Charleston in 1806, William Gilmore Simms is today regarded as the greatest southern man of letters of the nineteenth century. Writer Edgar Allan Poe once said that Simms displayed "more vigor, more imagination, more movement, more general capacity" than most other American writers combined. Simms published his first poems at age sixteen, and over his lifetime was the author of eighty-two books. His works include poetry, short stories, literary criticism, biographies (including his 1844 *Life of Francis Marion*), and numerous historical novels. *The Yemassee* (1835) is a fictional account of the Yamasee Indian war of 1715. His series of novels depicting South Carolina during the Revolutionary War began with *The Partisan*, published in 1835.

One of Simms's many protégés was Henry Timrod, known as the "poet laureate of the Confederacy." In 1866, he mourned the Confederate defeat in "Ode to the Dead in Magnolia Cemetery":

DuBose Heyward (right) immortalized Catfish Row (left) in his novel *Porgy*.

Stoop, angels, hither from the skies!
There is no holier spot of ground
Than where defeated valor lies
By mourning beauty crowned!

Penina Moise of Charleston published her first collection of poetry, *Fancy's Sketchbook*, in 1833, and continued to write throughout her long life. After she became totally blind, she dictated her poems to her niece. Penina Moise was a highly respected teacher, and the intellectuals of Charleston regularly attended her Friday-afternoon salons.

During the 1920s, Julia Peterkin wrote with grim realism about the poverty of blacks in South Carolina's Low Country. Her novel *Scarlet Sister Mary* won the Pulitzer Prize in fiction in 1929. The lives of the blacks who lived along Charleston's waterfront inspired DuBose Heyward's 1925 novel *Porgy*, the basis for George Gershwin's opera *Porgy and Bess*. Catfish Row, with its street vendors and dice games, brawls and romances, has become part of the American mystique.

Washington Allston (above) was noted for such Romantic paintings as *Moonlit Landscape* (right).

Contemporary writers also find rich material in South Carolina. Pat Conroy's autobiographical novel *The Water is Wide* is based on the experiences he had teaching black children in a two-room school on Daufuskie Island. Conroy's years as a student at The Citadel furnished the background for *The Lords of Discipline,* which became a popular movie. Another highly acclaimed South Carolina writer is Josephine Humphreys. Her novel *Dreams of Sleep,* a moving picture of class differences and the stresses of family life in modern Charleston, won the PEN/Hemingway Award in 1985.

FINE ARTS

In the days before photography, many American artists earned their living by painting portraits. One of the earliest South Carolina painters, and the first American woman artist to earn widespread recognition, was Henrietta Johnston. Johnston worked as a portrait painter in Charleston from 1708 until her death in 1728.

Born in 1779 on his family's plantation on the Waccamaw River, Washington Allston later studied at Harvard and in Europe. Eventually, he settled in Boston. Allston is regarded as the first American painter of the Romantic school. His landscapes convey nature in all its moods, both frightening and delightful. Allston exerted an enduring influence on nineteenth-century American painting, and today his works hang in the world's finest museums.

Thomas Sully moved to Charleston from England with his family when he was nine years old. Like Allston, he left South Carolina to study painting in Europe and never returned to his home state. Sully is best known for his portraits and historical paintings. One of his most famous works depicts George Washington just after he crossed the Delaware during the Revolutionary War.

A pioneer in American sculpture was Clark Mills, who began his life's work in Charleston around 1835. One of Mills's best-known sculptures is a marble bust of the fiery South Carolina statesman John C. Calhoun. Congress commissioned Mills to create a statue of President Andrew Jackson on horseback. Mills plunged into the work, though he had never seen the president or an equestrian statue. The work, which took years to complete, now graces the Andrew Jackson Monument in Washington, D.C.

Probably the most renowned South Carolina artist of the twentieth century is Jasper Johns. Born in Allendale in 1930, Johns became famous in the 1950s for his paintings of such familiar symbols as the American flag. In the 1960s, he became a leader of the pop art movement.

William Halsey of Charleston is a painter and sculptor who creates elaborate collages. Many of his abstract paintings remind viewers of the peeling paint of aging Charleston houses.

Contemporary South Carolina folk artists draw their inspiration from ethnic and cultural traditions. Sam Doyle of St. Helena Island began to paint when he was in his fifties. Using house paint on tin and plywood as his medium, he captures the harshness of life under slavery and the resilience of the black people who survived it. He also creates vibrant pictures of popular rock stars. Mary Jackson weaves sweet-grass baskets, a traditional handicraft of Low Country black women. Jackson's work, strong yet delicate, elevates basketmaking to an art form. Sarah Ayers, born on the Catawba reservation in 1919, is a master potter. Working in her studio in Columbia, she makes ceramic bowls and pitchers that express her Native American heritage.

PERFORMING ARTS

Since colonial days, South Carolinians have delighted in music, both classical and popular. The St. Cecilia Society, founded in Charleston in 1762, was the first musical society in America.

marching band
during Spoleto
Festival U.S.A.,
held annually
in Charleston

Every May and June, Charleston hosts Spoleto Festival U.S.A., an extravaganza of opera, orchestral music, jazz, theater, and films. Columbia supports a philharmonic orchestra, a youth orchestra, a choral society, and an opera company.

Country music is undoubtedly the most popular form of music in South Carolina, enjoyed by people of every generation. Gospel music, with its rich harmonies and lively renderings of beloved hymns, also flourishes in the state. Folklorists have collected hundreds of work songs, spirituals, and ballads from the Sea Islands, where blacks lived in relative isolation for centuries.

Founded in 1919, the Town Theater in Columbia is the oldest community theater in the United States. The University of South Carolina sponsors dramatic and musical-theater events throughout the year. In Charleston, playgoers attend the magnificent Dock Street Theater, built in 1736 and restored in 1938.

All the states have an official state bird, flower, and tree. But South Carolina is one of the only states in the nation that has an official state dance—a bouncy jitterbug called the Shag. In cities throughout the state, couples meet at Shag clubs to hop and twirl around the dance floor. The Shag evolved from an earlier dance known as the Big Apple, which originated in Columbia in the 1930s. The Big Apple became popular throughout the country, and the name of the dance eventually became New York City's nickname.

SPORTS

College football is a passion in South Carolina. The University of South Carolina Fighting Gamecocks and the Clemson Tigers are two excellent teams that enjoy devoted followings and have produced many outstanding professional athletes. All of South Carolina rejoiced in 1981 when the Clemson Tigers overwhelmed their opponents so resoundingly that they were named the nation's number-one college football team by the United Press International and Associated Press polls.

Although South Carolina has no major professional sports franchises, the state has spawned many professional athletes. Before the 1919 Black Sox Scandal cut short his career, "Shoeless

The Clemson Tigers
(in orange jerseys)

Joe'' Jackson of Greenville accumulated a lifetime batting average of .356. Larry Doby is another native South Carolinian who became a baseball star. In the late 1940s, Doby was the first black player in the American League, and three decades later he became the first black to manage an American League team. Bobby Richardson was voted the most outstanding player of the 1960 World Series and for several years was an all-star second baseman with the New York Yankees. Jim Rice, the slugging outfielder who starred with the Boston Red Sox in the 1980s, also hails from South Carolina. Alex English, a native of Columbia and a graduate of the University of South Carolina, is one of the all-time top ten scorers of the National Basketball Association. In addition to his basketball prowess, English is a published poet and an accomplished actor.

The excitement of auto racing thrills many South Carolina fans. The Southern 500, held annually in Darlington, is one of the country's most prestigious stock-car races. Stock-car races, extremely popular in the South, are contests among ordinary American-made sedans that have been altered to help them achieve incredible speeds.

Chapter 9
A BRIEF TOUR OF
THE PALMETTO STATE

A BRIEF TOUR OF THE PALMETTO STATE

"Smiling faces, beautiful places," proclaim South Carolina's glossy travel brochures, tempting visitors to discover the Palmetto State. The people of South Carolina are famous for their "southern hospitality." Smiling faces greet the visitor on city streets and along country roads—and every county has its beautiful places. South Carolina boasts glistening beaches and dazzling gardens; stately old houses and charming small towns. There are forty-seven state parks and historic sites, four state forests, and two national forests. A quick tour can touch upon only a few of the state's popular attractions and hidden surprises.

THE BLUE RIDGE AND THE PIEDMONT

Once the stronghold of the Cherokee Nation, the rugged Blue Ridge Mountains extend from North Carolina and Tennessee into the northwestern corner of South Carolina. The Blue Ridge is one of the most scenic areas of the state. The wild beauty of the mountains is protected in the Andrew Pickens Division of Sumter National Forest. Nearby, visitors can see the remains of the Stumphouse Mountain Tunnel. Part of an ambitious engineering project to create a rail link between Charleston and the Midwest, the tunnel was left unfinished with the outbreak of the Civil War.

Sassafras Mountain, near Table Rock State Park, is the highest point in the state. Climbers energetic enough to scale the

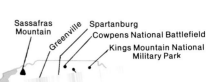

Dramatic rock formations are a feature of Peachtree Rock Nature Preserve in Lexington County.

mountain can enjoy the breathtaking view from the United States Forestry Department's lookout tower at the peak.

Gradually, the Blue Ridge Mountains descend into rolling foothills. Swift rivers tumbling from the mountainsides offered abundant waterpower for textile mills in the 1880s. The region is still heavily industrialized. Along Interstate 85, from Anderson to Spartanburg, commercial development is booming. The red clay where Scotch-Irish farmers once eked out their existence now sprouts suburban subdivisions and shopping malls. Greenville, sometimes called the textile center of the world, launched an elaborate revitalization program in 1981. Today, new hotels, office buildings, and a convention center cluster around the downtown plaza known as the Common. Greenville is also the home of Bob

Jones University. The university's Bibleland Museum houses the world's largest collection of sacred art and Biblical artifacts. The museum's planetarium places scientific phenomena within a Biblical framework.

Spartanburg, thirty miles (forty-eight kilometers) east of Greenville, is a growing industrial city that has attracted many foreign businesses. Visitors may hear German, French, or Japanese spoken on the streets. One of Spartanburg's finest attractions is Price House, a fully restored 1795 brick dwelling that once served as an inn for stagecoach travelers.

A landmark on the highway into Gaffney is the Peachoid, a 1-million-gallon (3.8-million-liter) water tower shaped like an enormous peach. Every July, Gaffney celebrates its annual Peach Festival. Through the sultry days of summer, roadside stands near the town tempt motorists to stop for a bag of the delicious, fuzzy-skinned fruit.

Two decisive battles of the Revolutionary War took place in the hills around Gaffney. Kings Mountain National Military Park commemorates the 1780 battle that broke British control over South Carolina. The march of the "overmountain men" and the siege of Ferguson's redcoats are re-created by amateur actors every year on October 7, the anniversary of the battle. The 1781 Battle of Cowpens, another important patriot victory, comes to life through slides and memorabilia at Cowpens National Battlefield.

Every April, the city of Rock Hill invites visitors to its week-long Come-See-Me Festival. During this special week, many of the town's elegant old homes are opened to the public. Visitors of all ages shriek with glee at the festival's frog-jumping contest. In the center of town lies Rock Hill's beloved Glencairn Gardens, several carefully tended acres of daffodils, periwinkles, myrtle, and boxwood, complete with a lily pond.

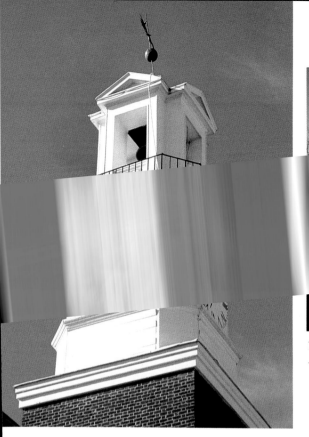

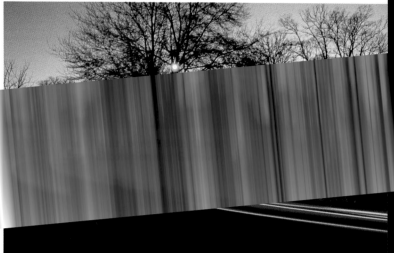

Left: The famous Winnsboro Town Clock
Above: Christmas decorations in Gaffney

South of Rock Hill lies the town of Winnsboro, the seat of Fairfield County. Hour after hour, since 1833, the Winnsboro Town Clock has faithfully tolled out the time. It is believed to be the oldest continuously running clock in the United States.

Along the Savannah River in the western part of the Piedmont spreads the Long Creek Division of Sumter National Forest. Amid the sand hills east of the forest lies the remarkable historic town of Edgefield. The Edgefield area has been home to no less than ten South Carolina governors, including "Pitchfork Ben" Tillman and Strom Thurmond.

CENTRAL SOUTH CAROLINA

The breeding and training of Thoroughbred horses is so popular in Aiken that the city has installed special stoplights at busy

Aiken, noted as a training center for Thoroughbred horses, holds hundreds of equestrian events throughout the year.

intersections for people on horseback. Horse lovers can spend many happy hours poring over racing memorabilia and portraits of champions in Aiken's Thoroughbred Hall of Fame.

A northeast journey along Interstate 20 brings one to the town of Lexington. The Lexington County Museum Complex, which traces the history of central South Carolina from 1772 to 1860, includes fifteen restored pre-Civil War buildings. Volunteers dressed in period costumes demonstrate spinning, weaving, and other almost-forgotten skills. Northwest of Lexington lies Lake Murray, a welcome refuge from the heat on scorching summer days.

The capital city of Columbia stands in the midst of South Carolina's Sand Hill country. Columbia is the state's largest city, as well as the business, financial, transportation, and education center of South Carolina. Modeled on the Capitol Building in Washington, D.C., South Carolina's State House is a proud survivor of General Sherman's assault on Columbia. Six bronze stars on the building's western wall mark where it was struck by Union cannonballs.

Among Columbia's other historic buildings is the Mann-Simons

Cottage. This white frame house, now a historical museum, was built in 1850 by a black woman from Charleston who [text obscured] freedom and walked to Colum[text obscured] Hampton. [text obscured]

[text obscured] parents are buried next to [text obscured] .esbyterian Church.

The University of South Carolina brings plays, concerts, and lectures to Columbia throughout the year. The McKissick Museum, on the university campus, includes art galleries and historical exhibits. On the first floor is the unique Movietonews Film Library, which preserves news films shot around the world from 1919 to 1963.

The people of Columbia are especially proud of the new South Carolina State Museum. Opened in 1988, it chronicles the history of the state in the areas of natural history, science and technology, cultural history, and art.

The Columbia Museum displays outstanding collections of Renaissance and Baroque art. The museum also features a "hands-on" children's gallery and a planetarium. The Confederate Relic Room and Museum overflows with Confederate uniforms, banners, currency, firearms, and sabers.

Opened in 1974, the Riverbanks Zoological Park is one of the most innovative zoos in the world. The zoo specializes in breeding endangered species and replaces traditional cages with re-creations of the animals' natural habitats. The zoo's rain-forest exhibit even features simulated tropical storms several times a day.

Columbia's Riverbanks Zoological Park features animals housed in naturalistic habitats.

Not far from the football stadium where the Fighting Gamecocks play is the State Farmers Market. A sprawling complex of indoor and outdoor stalls, it is the largest produce market in the southeastern United States. Farmers from all over the state bring their finest livestock, fruits, and vegetables to the South Carolina State Fair, hosted every year in Columbia during the third week of October.

Orangeburg, south of Columbia, is the gateway to the Low Country. Situated beside the North Edisto River, Orangeburg is the home of South Carolina State College. Along the riverbank are the lovely Edisto Memorial Gardens, which blossom luxuriantly with roses, wisteria, dogwood, and crepe myrtle.

South Carolina diplomat and statesman Joel Poinsett is buried in Stateburg, located east of Columbia. While serving as ambassador to Mexico in the 1820s, Poinsett fell in love with the beautiful flowers the Mexicans called the *noche buenas* and brought some back to the United States. In his honor, the Americans called the flowers *poinsettias*. Every Christmas, Poinsett's grave at the Church of the Holy Cross is ~~~~~~~~

~~~~~~~~~~~~~~~ level, the ground ~~~~~~~~ly and the trees are cloaked with the Spanish moss typical of the coastal plain.

THE PEE DEE COUNTRY

With its broad, tree-lined streets and handsome town square, Cheraw, in the northeastern part of the state, is one of South Carolina's most charming communities. During the early 1800s, Cheraw was a major commercial center. The waterfront, where steamboats were once loaded with cotton bound for northern ports, is now dotted with picnic tables and crowded with landings for pleasure craft. The cemetery around Old St. David's Episcopal Church is the final resting place of soldiers from every American war since the American Revolution. The cemetery's Confederate Monument, erected during the Reconstruction years, is the oldest monument to the Confederacy.

Devotees of stock-car racing won't want to miss Darlington, which hosts the Southern 500 NASCAR race every Labor Day weekend. The NMPA Stockcar Hall of Fame contains the world's largest collection of racing cars, including vehicles once driven by such stock-car greats as Fireball Roberts and Buddy Baker.

Florence, in the basin of the Pee Dee River, developed in the

Every year, Darlington hosts the exciting Southern 500 NASCAR race.

1850s as a railroad center. The Henry Timrod Park and Shrine marks the site of a one-room schoolhouse where the "poet laureate of the Confederacy" once taught. On the grounds of the Florence Airport stands the Florence Air and Missile Museum. Among the museum's displays is a genuine piece of moon rock.

The northeastern corner of the state is the heart of South Carolina's tobacco country. In such towns as Lamar, Lake City, and Dillon, tobacco warehouses stand along the sidewalks. Tobacco leaves are kept in these warehouses during the marketing season from July to September. The tobacco auctions held in these towns are intense, fast-paced events, for any dip or rise in the market may spell disaster or bonanza for the growers and merchants.

Myrtle
Beach

Murrells

Hilton Head Island

**Beautiful beaches are
a feature of the South
Carolina coast.**

THE COAST AND THE ISLANDS

Gleaming white sands stretch along South Carolina's northern coast from Cherry Grove Beach to Georgetown. Clumps of tall, graceful plants called sea oats help to anchor the sand against erosion from the wind and surf. The incredible width of these lovely beaches, many of which are lined with luxury hotels, has earned this part of the coast the nickname the Grand Strand. Even the names of the beaches sound cool and enticing on a hot summer day: Ocean Drive, Windy Hill, Surfside.

With its extensive golf courses, boats to rent for deep-sea fishing, and exquisite beaches for swimming and sunbathing, Myrtle Beach is the unofficial capital of the Grand Strand. It is also

Myrtle Beach is one of the most popular resorts along the Grand Strand.

the home of the South Carolina Hall of Fame, which pays tribute to South Carolinians who have made major contributions to American life. Among those honored are President Andrew Jackson, Vice-President John C. Calhoun, educator Mary McLeod Bethune, and astronaut Charles M. Duke.

Visitors to Murrells Inlet can tour the Hermitage, an 1842 house that is said to be haunted. According to legend, the ghost of a young woman named Alice, who died after a tragic love affair, still sets out from her home late at night to search the nearby marsh for her lost engagement ring. Not far from Murrells Inlet are South Carolina's unique Brookgreen Gardens. Scattered among beautifully tended shrubs and flowers are some four

Left: A sculpture at Brookgreen Gardens
Above: Prince George Winyah Church in Georgetown

hundred outdoor sculptures. Included are works by some of
America's finest sculptors, including Daniel Chester French and
Frederick Remington.

Georgetown, on Winyah Bay, is the site of the earliest white
settlement in South Carolina. The early colony's doomed
Spanish settlers left few traces, but Georgetown's later history
comes to life in the city's downtown historic district. Prince
George Winyah Episcopal Church was completed in 1750, and
the Man-Doyle House, built in 1775, was the town house of a
wealthy rice planter. The Rice Museum re-creates the history of
the rice and indigo trades, which once flourished in Georgetown
County.

South of Georgetown, the coast is broken by twisting inlets,
jutting capes, and barrier islands, which made it a nightmare for
early seamen. Ancient cypresses hung with curtains of Spanish

moss stand in the coastal marshes. With headquarters at Moore's Landing, Cape Romain National Wildlife Refuge preserves 60,000 acres (24,281 hectares) of salt marsh as a nesting ground for thousands of ducks, geese, herons, and other waterfowl. Further inland spreads the 245,000-acre (99,149-hectare) Francis Marion National Forest.

"Charleston is the spiritual center of the South," wrote one southern attorney. "Even an Atlantan will tell you that. Everybody in the South agrees Charleston is the best." Through wars, economic upheavals and vast social changes, Charleston has retained a quiet elegance. Old Charleston stands at the tip of the peninsula formed by the Ashley and Cooper rivers. At least 850 surviving buildings predate the Civil War, and many of them have been carefully restored. Members of some of Charleston's oldest and most prestigious families still live in this historic part of the city.

Today, cafes and boutiques line Catfish Row, where street vendors once sold strawberries and deviled crabs. Charleston's City Market, built in 1861, sells everything from produce to antiques.

In Charleston Harbor stands Fort Sumter, where the first shots of the Civil War resounded in 1861. Much of the old fort is open to the public, including gun rooms and enlisted men's barracks. The Fort Sumter Museum was dedicated on April 12, 1961, the hundredth anniversary of the battle.

The home of Revolutionary War hero William Henry Drayton still remains in the Drayton family after seven generations. Drayton Hall has been painstakingly restored. The gardens at nearby Middleton Place are perhaps Charleston's most popular tourist attraction. Begun in 1741, they are the nation's oldest formal landscaped gardens.

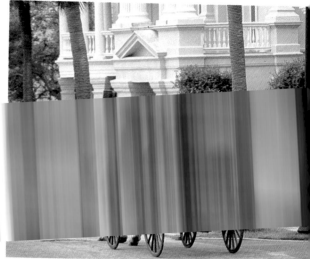

In Charleston, horse-drawn carriages (top right) take visitors along quaint streets lined with beautiful old homes and buildings (bottom right). Nearby are lovely Magnolia Gardens (top left) and historic Middleton Place (bottom left), which includes the nation's oldest formal landscaped gardens.

South of Charleston, the coast grows even more ragged, a tangle of inlets, cypress swamps, and marshy islands. Some of the islands, such as Edisto and Hilton Head, are popular resorts with hotels and condominiums overlooking the ocean. Despite the influx of tourism, the centuries-old culture of the Sea Islands still survives. Women still weave sweet-grass baskets, and older people can still be heard speaking Gullah, the unique language of this region.

The folklore and handcrafts of the Sea Islands are featured at the York W. Bailey Museum on St. Helena Island. The island's Penn School Museum commemorates the first school established for former slaves after the Civil War.

Thousands of young men from all over the country undergo rigorous boot-camp training at the Marine Corps Recruiting Depot on Parris Island. The Parris Island Museum contains exhibits relating to the island's history from 1564 to the present, including a collection of vintage Marine Corps uniforms and weapons. The Iwo Jima Flag-raising Monument is a tribute to the heroism of Marines in the Pacific during World War II.

Many splendid old homes stand in the beautiful waterfront city of Beaufort. The city's long and colorful history springs to life at the Beaufort Museum. Fossil displays remind visitors of the ancient creatures that once swam these waters and walked the land. The museum also features stone tools and pottery made by the Indians of the coast, bricks of tabby (a cementlike mixture made from lime, sand, and ground oyster shells that was used by the Spaniards in the 1500s), and rifles, cannonballs, uniforms, and other relics of the Civil War.

St. Helena's Episcopal Church in Beaufort served as a Civil War Hospital. According to legend, flat tombstones were hauled in from the churchyard to be used as operating tables.

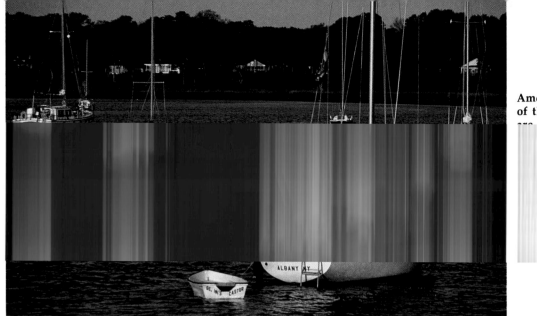

Among the highlights of the southern coast are Hilton Head Island

Port Royal, south of Beaufort, has been claimed by Indians, Spaniards, French Huguenots, English colonists, and American patriots. Above it have flown both the Confederate flag and the flag of the United States. Port Royal, which has witnessed so many scenes in the great pageant of South Carolina history, seems a fitting place to end the story of the Palmetto State.

GENERAL INFORMATION

Statehood: May 23, 1788, eighth state

Origin of Name: In 1629, the territory that included South Carolina and North Carolina was named *Carolana* (a Latin form of the name *Charles*) in honor of King Charles I of England. The spelling was changed to *Carolina* in the 1660s. South Carolina and North Carolina became separate colonies in 1712.

State Capital: Columbia, founded 1786

State Nickname: Palmetto State

State Flag: South Carolina's state flag, which originated during the Revolutionary War, was officially adopted in 1861. On a blue background appears a white palmetto, the state tree; and a white crescent. The crescent was an emblem that South Carolina soldiers wore on their caps during the Revolutionary War.

State Mottoes: Two Latin phrases: *Animis Opibusque Parati*, meaning "Prepared in mind and resources"; and *Dum Spiro Spero*, meaning "While I breathe, I hope"

State Bird: Carolina wren

State Flower: Carolina jessamine

State Tree: Palmetto

State Animal: White-tailed deer

State Fish: Striped bass

State Gemstone: Amethyst

State Stone: Blue granite

State Dance: The Shag

State Song: "Carolina," words by Henry Timrod, music by Anne Custis Burgess, adopted as the state song in 1911:

> The despot treads thy sacred sands,
> Thy pines give shelter to his bands;
> Thy sons stand by with idle hands,
> Carolina!
>
> He breathes at ease thy airs of balm,
> He scorns the lances of thy palm;
> Oh! who shall break thy craven calm,
> Carolina!
>
> Thy ancient fame is growing dim,
> A spot is on thy garment's rim;
> Give to the winds thy battle-hymn,
> Carolina!

POPULATION

Population: 3,122,814, twenty-fourth among the states

Population Density: 100 persons per sq. mi. (39 persons per km²)

Population Distribution: 54 percent of South Carolina's people live in cities or towns. Columbia, the state capital, is the largest city.

Columbia	101,229
Charleston	69,510
North Charleston	62,562
Greenville	58,242
Spartanburg	43,826
Rock Hill	35,327
Florence	30,062
Anderson	27,313
Sumter	24,890
Greenwood	21,613

(Population figures according to 1980 census)

Population Growth: South Carolina has experienced steady population growth over the years. Few European immigrants settled in South Carolina after the Revolutionary War, except for a short period during the early 1900s. Migration of black South Carolinians to the North after World War I kept the state's population stable for many years. Population growth increased more rapidly after 1960. Businesses moved to South Carolina from the North because of better climate, lower taxes, and lower wages. An increase in available jobs attracted workers from

1920	1,683,724
1940	1,899,804
1950	2,117,027
1960	2,382,594
1970	2,590,713
1980	3,122,814

GEOGRAPHY

Borders: South Carolina is bordered by North Carolina on the north and Georgia on the west. The Atlantic Ocean forms the eastern border.

Highest Point: Sassafras Mountain, 3,560 ft. (1,085 m)

Lowest Point: Sea level along the coast

Greatest Distances: North to south—218 mi. (351 km)
East to west—275 mi. (443 km)

Area: 31,113 sq. mi. (80,583 km²)

Rank in Area Among the States: Fortieth

Rivers: South Carolina is blessed with an excellent river system. During the early years, these rivers served as highways. The largest river, the Santee, drains about 40 percent of the state's area. The Pee Dee, South Carolina's second-largest river, flows through the eastern part of the state. The Savannah River forms the border with Georgia. Other major rivers include the Saluda, Ashley, Broad, Combahee, Edisto, and Cooper.

Lakes: South Carolina has no large inland lakes. The biggest lakes in the state are artificial lakes that were formed by dams. Lake Marion, the state's largest man-made lake, covers 173 sq. mi. (448 km²) and has a shoreline of 300 mi. (483 km).

Pitcher plants in Francis Marion National Forest

Other lakes include Greenwood and Murray on the Saluda River, Marion and Moultrie on the Santee River, Wylie and Wateree on the Wateree River, and Thurmond, Hartwell, and Russell on the Savannah River.

Coast: South Carolina's coastline would measure 187 mi. (301 km) if measured in a straight line. However, if all the coastal area were measured, the coastline would total 2,876 mi. (4,628 km). The northern part of the coast, from Little River Inlet to Winyah Bay, is nearly unbroken beach. South of Winyah Bay, much of the coastal area is covered by marshes.

Topography: South Carolina has three main land regions: the Atlantic Coastal Plain, the Piedmont, and the Blue Ridge. South Carolinians call the Atlantic Coastal Plain the Low Country. They refer to the Piedmont and the Blue Ridge as the Up Country.

The Atlantic Coastal Plain, which covers the eastern two-thirds of South Carolina, is divided into two regions. The Outer Coastal Plain extends 50 to 70 mi. (80 to 113 km) inland from the ocean. Swamps cover much of this flat land. The rolling, hilly Inner Coastal Plain contains a section of forested land called the Pine

Barrens. The western edge of the plain, which is characterized by high, sandy hills, is known as the Sand Hills region.

Between the Sand Hills and the Piedmont ...

... temperate in the hilly northwest ... subtropical along the coast. The northern part of the state has an average January temperature of 41° F. (5° C) and an average July temperature of 72° F. (22° C). The coastal region enjoys an average January temperature of 51° F. (10.5° C) and an average July temperature of 81° F. (27° C). The temperature soared to an all-time high of 111° F. (44° C) at Blackville on September 4, 1925; at Calhoun Falls on September 8, 1925; and at Camden on June 28, 1954. The lowest-recorded temperature was -20° F. (-29° C) at Caesar's Head on January 18, 1977. Precipitation is abundant and evenly distributed throughout the year. The northwest Blue Ridge region and the Atlantic coast receive the most precipitation.

NATURE

Trees: Forests cover nearly two-thirds of the state. South Carolina trees include oaks, laurels, hickories, magnolias, gums, pines, beeches, cypresses, hemlocks, maples, tulips, and redbuds.

Wild Plants: Palmetto, yucca, honeysuckle, Spanish moss, sweet bay, Venus's-flytrap, azalea, mountain laurel, rhododendron, pyxie, smilax, jessamine, gallberry, bay, dogwood

Animals: Deer, black bears, alligators, wildcats, shrews, opossums, raccoons, gray and red foxes, squirrels, rabbits, rattlesnakes, cottonmouths, water moccasins, turtles, salamanders, dolphins, sharks, sperm whales, sea turtles, shrimp, oysters, crabs

Birds: The 360 types of birds found in South Carolina include ducks, black skimmers, terns, pelicans, willets, plovers, oystercatchers, rails, egrets, herons, doves, snipes, woodcocks, mockingbirds, orioles, catbirds, warblers, vireos, wrens, sparrows, swallows, and thrushes.

Fish: South Carolina boasts about 350 kinds of saltwater fish, including sturgeon, shad, menhaden, flounder, sea bass, sea trout, drum, and grunt. The 70 kinds of freshwater fish include bass, bream, rockfish, and trout.

GOVERNMENT

South Carolina's government, like the federal government, is divided into legislative, executive, and judicial branches. The legislature, called the General Assembly, is made up of a senate and a house of representatives. The 46 members of the senate serve four-year terms. The 124 representatives of the house serve two-year terms. The General Assembly makes laws and determines how state revenue will be spent. It meets for one regular session each year, but the governor may call special sessions.

The governor is South Carolina's chief executive. South Carolinians also elect a lieutenant governor, attorney general, commissioner of agriculture, secretary of state, comptroller general, state treasurer, and superintendent of education. All executive-branch officials serve four-year terms. Until recently, the governor could not serve two consecutive terms.

Judicial power lies with the state supreme court. The supreme court has a chief justice and four associate justices who are elected to ten-year terms by the General Assembly. The General Assembly also elects sixteen circuit-court justices to four-year terms. Magistrates' courts hear minor civil and criminal cases. The governor appoints these judges with state senate approval. Most counties also have county courts that hear minor cases.

Number of Counties: 46

U.S. Representatives: 6

Electoral Votes: 8

Voting Qualifications: Eighteen years of age, registered to vote thirty days before the election

EDUCATION

Public education has long been important in South Carolina. Illiteracy was low during the early years because private schools appeared throughout the colony. The colonial government established semipublic schools called free schools in 1710. Poor children attended free, while others paid tuition. Lack of funds caused many of these schools to close. The state constitution of 1895 provided tax support for statewide public schools. For many years, South Carolina, like other southern states, maintained separate schools for blacks and whites. The U.S. Supreme Court ruled in 1954 that school segregation on the basis of race is unconstitutional. South Carolina began school integration in 1963.

A superintendent of schools and a state board of education head the public-school system. The board consists of one representative from each of the state's sixteen judicial districts and one representative chosen at large. Voters elect the superintendent to a four-year term.

South Carolina has twenty-seven colleges and universities. The largest is the University of South Carolina, which enrolls some twenty-three thousand students

A South Carolina paper mill

at its main campus in Columbia. The university also maintains campuses at Spartanburg, Aiken, Salkehatchie, Beaufort, Lancaster, and Sumter. Other schools in Columbia include Benedict College, Columbia Bible College, Columbia College, and Lutheran Theological Southern Seminary. Charleston is home to the Medical University of South Carolina; The Citadel, the Military College of South Carolina; College of Charleston; and Baptist College at Charleston. Other institutions of higher learning include Bob Jones University and Furman University, both in Greenville; Central Wesleyan College in Central; Claflin College and South Carolina State College, both in Orangeburg; Clemson University in Clemson; Coker College in Hartsville; Wofford College and Converse College, both in Spartanburg; Erskine College in Due West; Francis Marion College in Florence; Lander College in Greenwood; Limestone College in Gaffney; Morris College in Sumter; Newberry College in Newberry; Presbyterian College in Clinton; Voorhees College in Denmark; and Winthrop College in Rock Hill.

ECONOMY AND INDUSTRY

Principal Products:

Agriculture: Tobacco, soybeans, corn, peaches, cotton, apples, hay, oats, peanuts, berries, tomatoes, watermelons, asparagus, sweet potatoes, wheat, rye, eggs, dairy and beef cattle, sheep, hogs, broilers, turkeys, potatoes, cabbage, onions, pecans, sugarcane

Manufacturing: Textiles, chemicals, nonelectrical machinery, cottonseed products, lumber and forest products, clothing, paper products, rubber and plastics products, fabricated metal products

Natural Resources: Fertile soil, kaolin and other clays, sand and gravel, limestone, peat, granite, gold, mica, silica, talc, topaz, vermiculite, forests

Business: Manufacturing is an important part of South Carolina's economy. Manufactured goods such as textiles, chemicals, nonelectrical machinery, and clothing account for about 30 percent of the gross state product (GSP).

The government, including military services, is the most important service industry in the state. Military bases, especially those near Charleston, help make up 17 percent of the GSP. Wholesale and retail trade account for another 15 percent of the gross state product. Other service industries, including finance, insurance, transportation, communications, social services, and construction, make up 37 percent of the GSP.

Agriculture accounted for most of South Carolina's revenue in the years when cotton, rice, and indigo were the mainstay of the state's economy. Today, agriculture accounts for only 1 percent of the GSP. Tobacco, soybeans, and corn are the state's leading crops. South Carolina's fishing and mining industries make up less than 1 percent of the GSP.

Several of South Carolina's cities are regional trade centers. Columbia is a major farm-produce market. Greenville is a textile trade center. Charleston is an Atlantic trade port.

Communication: South Carolina's first newspaper, the *South Carolina Weekly Journal*, began publication in 1732 and lasted about six months. Today, about ninety-five newspapers, including about fifteen dailies, serve the state. The papers with the largest circulation include the *News and Courier* of Charleston, the *State* of Columbia, the *Anderson Independent-Mail*, the *Greenville News*, and the *Spartanburg Herald-Journal*.

South Carolina's first radio station, Spartanburg's WSPA, began broadcasting in 1930. The state's first television station, Columbia's WCOS-TV, opened in 1953. Today South Carolina has about 165 radio stations and about 30 television stations.

Transportation: Rivers were the "highways" of colonial South Carolina, and the Atlantic Intracoastal Waterway is an important inland shipping route, but roads, rails, and air lanes form the main transportation system today. South Carolina has about 63,000 mi. (101,386 km) of roads, including Interstate highways 20, 26, and 95. Railroads cover about 3,000 mi. (4,828 km) of track. Ten railroads provide freight and passenger service. South Carolina has about 75 public airports and 60 private airports. Charleston, Georgetown, and Port Royal are Atlantic seaports.

SOCIAL AND CULTURAL LIFE

Museums: South Carolina has treasured museums ever since its colonial days. The Charleston Museum, founded in 1773, is said to be the oldest museum in the United States. The museum features exhibits on South Carolina culture, anthropology, and colonial history. The recently opened South Carolina State Museum in Columbia, which features natural-history, science-and-technology, cultural-history, and art exhibits, is the state's finest museum. Other history museums include the South Carolina Historical Society and the Old Powder Magazine in Charleston, and the South Carolina Confederate Relic Room and Museum in Columbia. South Carolina has many art museums, including the

Columbia Museum of Art, the Greenville County Museum of Art in Greenville, and the Gibbes Art Gallery in Charleston. Bob Jones University in Greenville has a museum that houses a large collection of religious art. Lexington County Museum, near Lexington, is a re-creation of a colonial village. Brookgreen Gardens, near Georgetown, is an outdoor museum known for its sculptures.

Libraries: The first public library in the thirteen colonies was opened in Charleston in 1698. The South Caroliniana Library on the University of South Carolina campus at Columbia, built in 1840, was the nation's first separate college library.

Today, South Carolina has an extensive library system of about forty county or multicounty (regional) libraries. Bookmobiles travel from these libraries to serve isolated areas. The state also has many state and university libraries.

Performing Arts: Performing arts have long been important in South Carolina. Charleston is the home of the Dock Street Theater, built in 1736. It was the first building in the United States constructed solely for use as a theater. The Town Theater in Columbia is one of the oldest little theaters in the United States. South

Carolina boasts symphony orchestras in Columbia, Greenville, and Charleston, as well as chamber music groups and choral societies in several cities. Spoleto Festival U.S.A. in Charleston is an annual festival of music, dance, and theater.

Sports and Recreation: South Carolina has no major professional sports teams. However, South Carolinians are football fanatics. The Clemson University Tigers, in the powerful Atlantic Coast Conference, were named the number-one college football team in 1981. The University of South Carolina Fighting Gamecocks also have a strong following. Auto racing is the other important spectator sport in South Carolina. Thousands of South Carolinians come to Darlington to see the Transouth 500 Stock Car Race in early April and the Southern 500 on Labor Day weekend.

South Carolinians who enjoy the outdoors may hike or camp in the state's two national forests. Francis Marion Forest in Berkeley and Charleston counties covers 245,000 acres (99,149 hectares). Sumter National Forest, which includes the Andrew Pickens Division in the Blue Ridge and the Long Creek and Enoree divisions in the Piedmont, covers a total of 350,000 acres (141,642 hectares). The state also has two state forests and more than forty-seven state parks and historical areas. Hunters may pursue quail, turkey, pheasant, goose, deer, and rabbit. Fishermen enjoy catching bass, bream, crappie, trout, and many other kinds of fish.

Historic Sites and Landmarks:

Charles Towne Landing, near Charleston, is the site of the first permanent English settlement in South Carolina. It includes beautiful English-park-style gardens, reproductions of seventeenth-century buildings and a seventeenth-century trading ship, a 1670 garden showing crops grown by the early settlers, and a forest populated with animals native to South Carolina in the 1600s.

Cowpens National Battlefield, near Gaffney, was the scene of an important patriot victory over the British in 1781.

Fort Hill, on the Clemson University campus, was the longtime home of John C. Calhoun. Built in the early 1800s, this National Historic Landmark features many original furnishings.

Fort Moultrie National Monument, on Sullivan's Island, is where, in 1776, American Colonel William Moultrie and his men drove off a squadron of British warships in what was the first decisive battle of the Revolutionary War.

Fort Sumter National Monument, in Charleston Harbor, is where the first shots of the Civil War were fired in 1861.

Georgetown Historic District, in Georgetown, features restored nineteenth-century storefronts, homes, churches, and a riverwalk.

Hampton-Preston Mansion and Garden, in Columbia, is a restored 1820s mansion that at separate times was home to two of South Carolina's most distinguished families.

Historic Camden, near Camden, is a Revolutionary War park on the site of the early village of Camden. The site includes several restored buildings from the Revolutionary period, including the Kershaw House, which served as the headquarters for British General Cornwallis.

Kings Mountain National Military Park, near York, is the site of a battle that is said to have been a turning point in the Revolutionary War. Here, in 1780, the British were defeated by outnumbered and ill-equipped colonists. The park includes the battlefield, monuments, and a museum.

Robert Mills Historic House and Park, in Columbia, is a restored 1823 mansion that was designed by Robert Mills, architect of the Washington Monument.

Ninety Six National Historic Site, near Ninety Six, is the site of the first Revolutionary War battle in South Carolina.

Old Dorchester State Park, near Summerville, contains the ruins of an eighteenth-century town. The old fort at the site withstood many skirmishes during the Revolutionary War.

Old Exchange and Provost Dungeon, near Charleston, served as an important meeting place for American patriots in the 1770s. The Provost Dungeon, underneath the Exchange Building, was used as a British prison during the Revolutionary War.

Pendleton Historical and Recreational District is one of the largest historic districts in the nation. The district, which includes the Scotch-Irish community of Pendleton and a three-county area, offers many historical and scenic attractions, including many beautiful restored homes, a museum of antique farming equipment, and the nation's oldest farmers' hall in continuous use.

The Avenue of Oaks at Boone Hall Plantation near Charleston

Sheldon Church Ruins, near Gardens Corner, are the ruins of a church that was built in the mid-1700s, burned by the British during the Revolutionary War, rebuilt in 1826, and then burned again by the troops of General Sherman in 1865.

Woodrow Wilson Home, in Columbia, was a boyhood home of the twenty-eighth president of the United States.

Other Interesting Places to Visit:

Boone Hall Plantation, at Mount Pleasant, was one of the grandest plantations of the colonial era. Originally comprising 17,000 acres (6,880 hectares), it was the home of Major John Boone, a member of Charles Towne's first group of settlers.

Cape Romain National Wildlife Refuge, on Bulls Island, is a wild stretch of barrier islands and salt marshes that is the home of hundreds of species of birds.

Carolina Sandhills National Wildlife Refuge, in Chesterfield County, contains dunes that millions of years ago were the shore of an ancient ocean. The sanctuary supports many wildlife species, including the largest population of red-cockaded woodpeckers found on any refuge.

Carowinds, in York County, is a theme park and amphitheater offering rides, shows, restaurants, and shops.

Cherokee Foothills Sce

...memorial Gardens, in Orangeburg, is a city-owned display of azaleas, camellias, roses, and other flowers.

Governor's Mansion, in Columbia, has been the home of the state's chief executive since 1868.

Hilton Head Island, on the Atlantic coast, is one of the nation's most famous resorts. This island is known for its beautiful, wide beaches, and for its reputation as a tennis and golf center.

Landsford Canal State Park, near Lancaster, shows visitors the canal system that once served as a major transportation system in South Carolina.

Magnolia Plantation and Gardens, near Charleston, was the home of ten generations of the Drayton family. Visitors may tour the nation's oldest colonial estate garden and the Reconstruction-era plantation house that rises on the original foundation.

Memorial Park, in Columbia, is the largest Vietnam War monument of its type outside of Washington, D.C.

Middleton Place, near Charleston, is the eighteenth-century river plantation and home of Henry Middleton, president of the First Continental Congress. The plantation includes America's oldest formal landscaped gardens.

Pawleys Island, along the Grand Strand, offers weathered inns and vast fields of marsh grass. Visitors can watch local craftsmen make the woven-cord hammocks for which the island is famous.

South Carolina Hall of Fame, in Myrtle Beach, honors many of the state's most influential sons and daughters.

State House, in Columbia, completed in 1868, houses the Governor's Office and the General Assembly.

IMPORTANT DATES

1521—Spaniard Francisco Gordillo explores the Carolina coast

1526—Lucas Vásquez de Ayllón, an explorer from Santo Domingo, attempts to establish a colony on the Carolina coast

1562—French Huguenots establish a short-lived colony at Port Royal

1629—King Charles I of England grants a tract of North American land—including the land of present-day North Carolina and South Carolina—to Sir Robert Heath, who names it *Carolana* after the monarch

1663—King Charles II grants Carolana (now renamed Carolina) to eight English noblemen who become the lords proprietors

1670—English settlers sent by the lords proprietors establish Albemarle Point, the first permanent white settlement in South Carolina

1680—The colonists move to Oyster Point and establish Charles Towne (since 1783 spelled Charleston)

1698—The first government-supported lending library in the American colonies is opened in Charles Towne

1710—The northern and southern sections of the Carolina Colony become administered by separate governors; the colonial government establishes free schools for poor children

1712—South Carolina and North Carolina become separate colonies

1715—After Yamasee Indians try to drive colonists from Carolina, colonists defeat the Indians in what becomes known as the Yamasee War

1719—The colonists ask the British government to abolish proprietary rule; King George I accepts their request, declares South Carolina a royal colony, and allows the colonists to govern themselves

1729—The British government buys the property rights of the lords proprietors, and South Carolina officially becomes a royal colony ruled directly by the king

1732—The southern part of South Carolina becomes the colony of Georgia

1744—Eliza Lucas introduces indigo to South Carolina

1762—Charlestonians establish the St. Cecilia Society, the first musical society in America

1769—Circuit courts are established throughout the South Carolina colony

1773—The Charleston Library Society opens the first
colonies

...ge, colonial American
...ountain, one of the turning points of the
...onary War

1781—Colonial forces win the Battle of Cowpens, giving the British their most
devastating defeat of the southern campaign

1782—The British evacuate Charles Towne

1788—South Carolina joins the Union as the eighth state

1790—Columbia replaces Charleston as South Carolina's state capital

1793—Eli Whitney patents the cotton gin, revolutionizing agriculture in the South

1800—The Santee Canal is completed, linking Charleston with the Santee River
system

1801—South Carolina College (now the University of South Carolina) opens at
Columbia

1817—South Carolina native John C. Calhoun is named U.S. secretary of war

1822—A slave rebellion planned by Denmark Vesey is prevented from occurring

1824—John C. Calhoun is elected vice-president of the United States; The Citadel,
South Carolina's military college, is founded

1826—The Fireproof Building, the nation's first building of fireproof construction,
is completed

1828—South Carolina native Andrew Jackson is elected president of the United
States

1830—*Best Friend of Charleston*, the first steam locomotive to be placed in regular
passenger and freight service, makes its first run; the world's first department
store is established at King and Market Streets in Charleston

1832—South Carolina opposes the federal tariff and passes the Ordinance of Nullification; Calhoun resigns as vice-president to enter the Senate

1837—South Carolina native Joel R. Poinsett is named U.S. secretary of war

1847—South Carolina native Pierce M. Butler's Palmetto Regiment plays a leading role in capturing Mexico City and winning the Mexican War

1860—South Carolina becomes the first state to secede from the Union

1861—Confederate troops fire on Charleston's Fort Sumter, beginning the Civil War

1865—Union General William Tecumseh Sherman's troops devastate Columbia

1868—South Carolina is readmitted to the Union

1876—Democrats regain control of the South Carolina legislature

1877—Reconstruction ends in South Carolina

1886—Ninety-two persons die during an earthquake in Charleston

1890—Populist Governor "Pitchfork Ben" Tillman begins agricultural and vocational education reforms; Charles Shepherd establishes the first commercial tea farm in the United States

1893—A coastal hurricane kills more than a thousand South Carolinians

1895—South Carolina adopts a new constitution

1921—Boll weevils destroy half of South Carolina's cotton crop

1929—The South Carolina State Highway Department begins a statewide highway-building program

1938—The state legislature enacts a forty-hour workweek for textile workers

1941—The newly completed Santee Dam harnesses the Santee River to provide the state's first hydroelectric power

1948—Governor Strom Thurmond runs for president of the United States as the candidate of the States' Rights Democratic ("Dixiecrat") party

1953—The Savannah River Plant, South Carolina's first nuclear energy plant, opens near Aiken

1963—Harvey Gantt becomes the first black student to enter Clemson University; South Carolina's public schools begin integration

1964—Barry Goldwater becomes the first Republican presidential candidate to
   carry South Carolina since Reconstruction; Democratic Senator Strom
   Thurmond switches to the Republican P̶.

.... i. DeQuincey Newman becomes the first black elected to the
state senate since the 1870s

IMPORTANT PEOPLE

Washington Allston (1779-1843), born in Georgetown County;
   artist; led American painters in the Romantic tradition of the
   1800s; best-known works include *Moonlit Landscape* and
   Belshazzar's Feast

Sara Ayers (1919-   ), born on the Catawba Indian Reservation;
   artist; potter who uses contemporary themes and Indian
   traditions

Bernard Mannes Baruch (1870-1965), born in Camden; financier,
   philanthropist, statesman; served as chairman of the War
   Industries Board during World War I; advised every U.S.
   president from Woodrow Wilson to Dwight Eisenhower

Joseph Louis Cardinal Bernardin (1928-   ), born in Columbia;
   Catholic clergyman; became Archbishop of Chicago in 1982;
   appointed a cardinal in 1983; received the Einstein Peace Prize for
   his advocacy of nuclear disarmament

Mary McLeod Bethune (1875-1955), born in Mayesville; educator;
   worked to improve educational opportunities for blacks; founded
   Bethune-Cookman College in Florida and the National Council of
   Negro Women; advised U.S. presidents from Calvin Coolidge to
   Harry Truman

BERNARD BARUCH

MARY McLEOD BETHUNE

PIERCE BUTLER

JAMES BYRNES

PAT CONROY

ANNE CUNNINGHAM

Pierce Butler (1744-1822), planter, Revolutionary War patriot, politician; born in Ireland, he came to South Carolina in the 1760s while serving in the British army; resigned to become a planter; became a leader in the American Revolutionary cause; signer of the U.S. Constitution; as a member of the Constitutional Convention of 1787, supported the checks and balances system and the electoral college; first U.S. senator from South Carolina (1789-96, 1803, 1804)

James Francis Byrnes (1879-1972), born in Charleston; politician; U.S. representative (1911-25); U.S. senator (1931-41); associate justice of the U.S. Supreme Court (1941-42); U.S. secretary of state under Harry Truman (1945-47); governor of South Carolina (1951-55)

John Caldwell Calhoun (1782-1850), born in Abbeville; politician; U.S. representative (1811-17); was called a "War Hawk" because he advocated the War of 1812; U.S. secretary of war (1817-25); vice-president under John Quincy Adams and Andrew Jackson (1825-32); champion of states' rights; leader of South Carolina's nullification movement; resigned as vice-president to enter the Senate (1833-43); U.S. secretary of state (1844-45); U.S. senator (1845-50)

Thomas Green Clemson (1807-1888), engineer, educator; worked to promote agricultural colleges; willed most of his estate to the state of South Carolina for the founding of an agricultural school (Clemson College, now Clemson University, chartered 1889)

David Coker (1870-1938), born in Hartsville; agriculturalist; bred cotton to produce larger and better strains

Pat Conroy (1945-   ), writer; best known for such semiautobiographical and South Carolina-based works as *The Water is Wide*, *The Lords of Discipline*, and *The Great Santini*, all of which were adapted into popular movies

Anne Pamela Cunningham (1816-1875), born in Laurens County; preservationist; directed the restoration of the George Washington mansion at Mount Vernon

Lawrence Doby (1923-   ), born in Camden; baseball player; became the first black player in the American League when he joined the Cleveland Indians in 1947; led the Indians to pennants in 1948 and 1954; twice led the league in home runs and runs batted in; became the first black manager of the American League in 1978

Charles Fraser (1782-1860), born in Charleston; artist; painted more than 300 miniatures and 139 paintings; influenced many other artists who came to Charleston at the time when it was considered by many to be the "cultural center of America"

Christopher Gadsden (1724-1805), born in Charleston; Revolutionary War patriot; known as the "Flame of Liberty"; radical leader who pushed for revolt against the British; delegate to the Continental Congress (1774-76); brigadier in the Continental army (1...

...Gildersleeve (1831-1924), born in Charleston; educator, philologist; professor of Greek at the University of Virginia and Johns Hopkins University; founded and edited *The American Journal of Philology* (1880-1920)

John Birks (Dizzy) Gillespie (1917-   ), born in Cheraw; trumpet player, composer; played with Cab Calloway and Duke Ellington before forming his own band; helped create the "bebop" style of jazz; became known as "King of Bebop"

Will Lou Gray (1883-1984), born in Laurens; educator; persuaded the South Carolina state legislature to form the State Illiteracy Commission; later led the State Department of Adult Education; promoted the motto, "Why Stop Learning?"

Angelina Emily Grimké (1805-1879), born in Charleston; abolitionist, supporter of women's rights; she and her sister Sarah lectured in the northeastern states on behalf of the American Anti-Slavery Society; both sisters also took up the cause of women's rights after receiving negative responses to their participation in the abolitionist movement; wrote the antislavery pamphlet *Appeal to the Christian Women of the South*

Sarah Moore Grimké (1792-1873), born in Charleston; abolitionist, women's rights advocate; lectured on the evils of slavery; wrote one of the first American essays on women's equality, *Letters on the Equality of the Sexes and the Condition of Women*

William Stone Hall (1915-   ), born in Wagener; physician; studied the plight of the mentally ill and directed the South Carolina Department of Mental Health (1963-85), one of the largest state mental-health departments in the Southeast

William Halsey (1915-   ), born in Charleston; artist; gained fame as an abstract painter and sculptor; creates many works of art from Mayan designs; creates many works about children

Wade Hampton (1818-1902), born in Charleston; military officer, politician; illustrious Confederate general; governor of South Carolina (1876-79); U.S. senator (1879-91)

ALTHEA GIBSON

DIZZY GILLESPIE

WADE HAMPTON

127

THOMAS HEYWARD

ERNEST HOLLINGS

JESSE JACKSON

CLARA LOUISE KELLOGG

Robert Young Hayne (1731-1839), born in Colleton District; politician; U.S. senator (1823-32); states' rights advocate and one of the leaders of the nullification movement; debated Daniel Webster over the issue of states' rights; governor of South Carolina (1832-34)

Edwin DuBose Heyward (1885-1940), born in Charleston; poet and author; his novel *Porgy* was adapted into the famed George Gershwin opera *Porgy and Bess*

Thomas Heyward (1746-1809), born in St. Luke's Parish; soldier, American Revolutionary patriot, politician; member of the Continental Congress (1776-78); signer of the Declaration of Independence; served as first president of the South Carolina Agricultural Society

Ernest "Fritz" Hollings (1922-   ), born in Charleston; politician; governor of South Carolina (1959-63); U.S. senator (1966-   ); chairman of the Senate Commerce Committee

Josephine Humphreys (1945-   ), born in Charleston; writer; won 1985 PEN/Hemingway Award for *Dreams of Sleep*

Anna Hyatt Huntington (1876-1973); sculptor, artist; developed Brookgreen Gardens, the world's largest outdoor sculpture gardens

Andrew Jackson (1767-1845), born in Waxhaw; seventh president of the United States (1829-1837); became a national military hero after defeating the British in the 1815 Battle of New Orleans; became the first "common man" to be elected president; upheld national sovereignty during the South Carolina nullification crisis

Jesse Jackson (1941-   ), born in Greenville; Baptist minister, civil-rights leader, politician; known for his stirring speeches; director of Operation Breadbasket (1966-71); founded the organization People United to Serve Humanity (PUSH) (1971); candidate for the Democratic presidential nomination in 1984 and 1988

Clara Louise Kellogg (1842-1916), born in Sumter; singer; became known as South Carolina's most illustrious prima donna; attained fame in America and Europe

Lane Kirkland (1922-   ), born in Camden; labor leader; president of the American Federation of Labor and Congress of Industrial Organizations (AFL-CIO) (1979-   )

Eartha Kitt (1928-   ), born in North; singer and actress; combined jazzy and popular styles in her music; known for her renditions of "C'est Si Bon " and "Blues"

Henry Laurens (1724-1792), born in Charleston; diplomat; member and president (1777-78) of the Continental Congress (1777-79); negotiated the peace treaty with Great Britain that ended the Revolutionary War

James Longstreet (1821-1904), born in Edgefield District; military officer; Confederate general; led Confederate troops in most of the major battles of northern Virginia; U.S. minister to Turkey (1880-81); U.S. marshal (1881-84); U.S. ...

... nyan; military leader; ... Cherokee Indians (1759, 1761); the guerrilla tactics he used while commanding South Carolina militia during the Revolutionary War earned him the nickname the "Swamp Fox"; rescued Americans surrounded by the British at Parkers Ferry (1781); named brigadier general (1781)

Benjamin Elijah Mays (1894-1984), born in Epworth; Baptist minister, educator; dean of the School of Religion at Harvard University (1934-40); president of Morehouse College (1940-67); received the NAACP Spingarn Medal (1982)

Vardry McBee (1775-1864), born in Spartanburg; planter; called the "Father of Greenville"; secured the city's first cotton mill and railroad depot

Arthur Middleton (1742-1787), born near Charleston; statesman; member of the Continental Congress (1776-78, 1781-83); signer of the Declaration of Independence; designed the South Carolina state seal

Robert Mills (1751-1855), born in Charleston; architect; considered the nation's first professional architect; designed the Washington Monument, the Treasury Building, the Patent Office, and more than fifty other Washington, D.C., buildings

Penina Moise (1797-1880), born in Charleston; poet; published *Fancy's Sketch Book* and *Hymns for the Use of Hebrew Congregations*

William Moultrie (1730-1805), born in Charleston; American Revolutionary general, politician; defended Charleston against a British fleet in 1776; governor of South Carolina (1785-87, 1792-94)

Mary Simms Oliphant (1891-   ), born in Barnwell; historian; wrote fifteen volumes describing the state's history

Julia Mood Peterkin (1880-1961), born in Laurens County; novelist; noted for her depiction of the lives of black South Carolinians; won the 1929 Pulitzer Prize in fiction for *Scarlet Sister Mary*

FRANCIS MARION

BENJAMIN MAYS

JULIA PETERKIN

JAMES PETIGRU

ANDREW PICKENS

THOMAS PINCKNEY

JOEL POINSETT

James Louis Petigru (1789-1863), born in Abbeville District; lawyer, politician; Unionist who ardently opposed the South Carolina secessionist movement, but continued to live in Charleston after the Confederacy was established

Andrew Pickens (1739-1817); Revolutionary War commander; distinguished himself in many Revolutionary War battles, including the decisive Battle of Cowpens

Charles Pinckney (1757-1824), born in Charleston; politician, diplomat; member of the Continental Congress (1784-87); delegate to the Constitutional Convention (1787); one of the principal architects of the U.S. Constitution; governor of South Carolina (1789-92, 1796-98, 1806-08); U.S. senator (1798-1801); U.S. minister to Spain (1801-05); U.S. representative (1819-21)

Charles Cotesworth Pinckney (1746-1825), born in Charleston; cousin of Charles Pinckney; Revolutionary War patriot and soldier, diplomat; delegate to the Constitutional Convention (1787); minister to France (1796) (though not recognized by France); led the movement to create South Carolina College (now the University of South Carolina)

Eliza Lucas Pinckney (1722-1793); mother of Charles Cotesworth Pinckney; planter; came to South Carolina in 1738; introduced indigo cultivation in South Carolina

Thomas Pinckney (1750-1828), born in Charleston; son of Eliza Lucas Pinckney; soldier, politician, diplomat; governor of South Carolina (1787-89); U.S. minister to Great Britain (1792-94); arranged the 1795 Treaty of San Lorenzo with Spain, which eased tensions between the U.S. and Florida by settling the U.S.-Spanish boundary line; U.S. representative (1797-1801); general in the War of 1812

Joel Roberts Poinsett (1779-1851), born in Charleston; politician, diplomat, traveler; U.S. representative (1821-25); U.S. minister to Mexico (1825-29); U.S. secretary of war (1837-41); introduced the poinsettia plant (named in his honor) from Mexico to the United States

James Edward (Jim) Rice (1953-   ), born in Anderson; professional baseball player; helped lead the Boston Red Sox to pennants in 1975 and 1986; his slugging earned him the American League Most Valuable Player Award in 1978

Robert Clinton (Bobby) Richardson (1935-   ), born in Sumter; professional baseball player; starred at second base with the New York Yankees; named many times to the American League All-Star team; named Most Valuable Player of the 1960 World Series

Archibald D. Rutledge (1883-1973), born in McClellanville; poet laureate of South Carolina (1934); wrote 90 books and more than six thousand poems, many of which honored South Carolina

John Rutledge (1739-1800), born in Charleston; Revolutionary War patriot and soldier, politician; member of the Continental Congress (1774-76, 1782-83); first state governor of South Carolina (1776-78, 177...

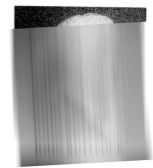

...g forced into the Confederate navy, commandeered a Confederate messenger ship, sailed it through Charleston Harbor, and delivered it into Union hands (1862); became the highest-ranked black officer in the Union navy; U.S. representative (1875-79, 1882-87)

Thomas Sumter (1734-1832); military officer, politician; settled in South Carolina in 1765; led guerrilla-type campaigns against the British in South Carolina during the Revolutionary War; became known as the "Gamecock"; U.S. representative (1789-93, 1797-1801); U.S. senator (1801-10)

James (Strom) Thurmond (1902-   ), born in Edgefield; politician; governor of South Carolina (1947-51); States' Rights Democratic ("Dixiecrat") presidential candidate (1948); U.S. senator (1955-   ); energized the Republican party in South Carolina when he switched from the Democratic party in 1964

Benjamin Ryan Tillman (1847-1918), nicknamed "Pitchfork Ben"; born in Edgefield County; politician; governor of South Carolina (1890-94); as governor, championed the small farmer, favored educational reform, and helped establish state constitution of 1895; U.S. senator (1895-1918)

Henry Timrod (1829-1867), born in Charleston; poet, teacher; taught and wrote throughout the state; was considered the "poet laureate of the Confederacy"; among his famous poems are "Ode to the Cotton Boll" and "Ode to the Dead in Magnolia Cemetery"

Charles H. Townes (1915-   ), born in Greenville; physicist; won the 1964 Nobel Prize in physics for his research on lasers

Denmark Vesey (1767?-1822), former slave who planned an unsuccessful slave revolt in South Carolina

John B. Watson (1878-1958), born in Greenville; psychologist; pioneered the school of psychology known as behaviorism

William Caleb (Cale) Yarborough (1939-   ), born in Timmonsville; professional race-car driver; NASCAR (National Association for Stock Car Racing) Grand National Champion in 1976, 1977, and 1978

BENJAMIN TILLMAN

HENRY TIMROD

JOHN WATSON

GOVERNORS

John Rutledge	1776-1778	James L. Orr	1865-1868
Rawlins Lowndes	1778-1779	Robert K. Scott	1868-1872
John Rutledge	1779-1782	Franklin J. Moses, Jr.	1872-1874
John Mathews	1782-1783	Daniel H. Chamberlain	1874-1876
Benjamin Guerard	1783-1785	Wade Hampton	1876-1879
William Moultrie	1785-1787	William D. Simpson	1879-1880
Thomas Pinckney	1787-1789	Thomas B. Jeter	1880
Charles Pinckney	1789-1792	Johnson Hagood	1880-1882
William Moultrie	1792-1794	Hugh S. Thompson	1882-1886
Arnoldus Vander Horst	1794-1796	John C. Sheppard	1886
Charles Pinckney	1796-1798	John P. Richardson	1886-1890
Edward Rutledge	1798-1800	Benjamin R. Tillman	1890-1894
John Drayton	1800-1802	John G. Evans	1894-1897
James B. Richardson	1802-1804	William H. Ellerbe	1897-1899
Paul Hamilton	1804-1806	Miles B. McSweeney	1899-1903
Charles Pinckney	1806-1808	Duncan C. Heyward	1903-1907
John Drayton	1808-1810	Martin F. Ansel	1907-1911
Henry Middleton	1810-1812	Coleman L. Blease	1911-1915
Joseph Alston	1812-1814	Charles A. Smith	1915
David R. Williams	1814-1816	Richard I. Manning	1915-1919
Andrew Pickens	1816-1818	Robert A. Cooper	1919-1922
John Geddes	1818-1820	Wilson G. Harvey	1922-1923
Thomas Bennett	1820-1822	Thomas G. McLeod	1923-1927
John L. Wilson	1822-1824	John G. Richards	1927-1931
Richard I. Manning	1824-1826	Ibra C. Blackwood	1931-1935
John Taylor	1826-1828	Olin D. Johnston	1935-1939
Stephen D. Miller	1828-1830	Burnet R. Maybank	1939-1941
James Hamilton, Jr.	1830-1832	J. Emile Harley	1941-1942
Robert Y. Hayne	1832-1834	Richard M. Jefferies	1942-1943
George McDuffie	1834-1836	Olin D. Johnston	1943-1945
Pierce M. Butler	1836-1838	Ransome J. Williams	1945-1947
Patrick Noble	1838-1840	J. Strom Thurmond	1947-1951
B.K. Henagan	1840	James F. Byrnes	1951-1955
John P. Richardson	1840-1842	George B. Timmerman, Jr.	1955-1959
James H. Hammond	1842-1844	Ernest F. Hollings	1959-1963
William Aiken	1844-1846	Donald S. Russell	1963-1965
David Johnson	1846-1848	Robert E. McNair	1965-1971
Whitemarsh B. Seabrook	1848-1850	John C. West	1971-1975
John H. Means	1850-1852	James B. Edwards	1975-1979
John L. Manning	1852-1854	Richard W. Riley	1979-1987
James H. Adams	1854-1856	Carroll A. Campbell, Jr.	1987-
Robert F.W. Allston	1856-1858		
William H. Gist	1858-1860		
Francis W. Pickens	1860-1862		
Milledge L. Bonham	1862-1864		
Andrew G. Magrath	1864-1865		
Benjamin F. Perry	1865		

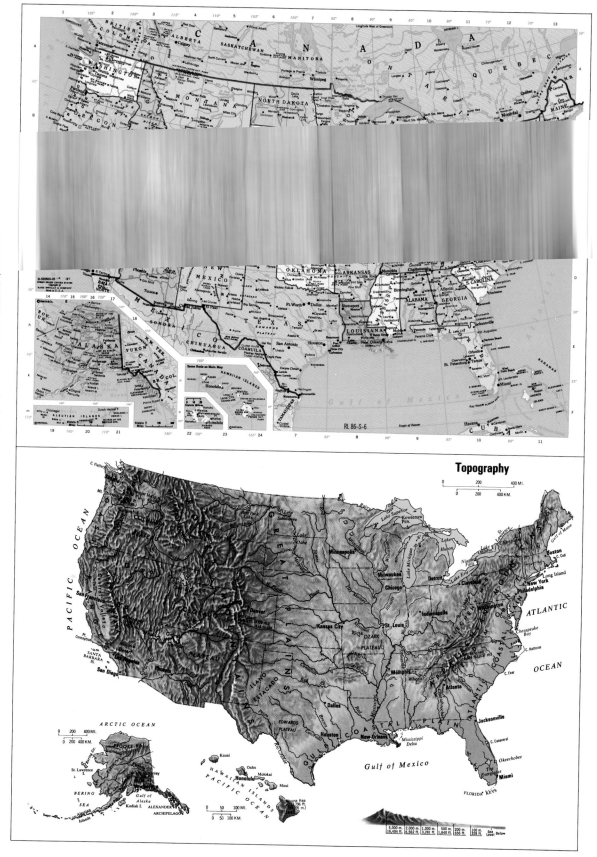

RL 86-S-6

Topography

MAP KEY

Index

Abbeville C3
Adams Run k11
Aiken D4
Alcolu D7
Allendale E5
Anderson B2
Andrews E8
Arcadia B4
Arlington B3
Ashepoo River (river) F6
Ashley River (river) F7
Amor D9
Back River (river) h12
Bailey Island k11
Baldwin Mills B5
Bamberg E5
Barnwell E5
Batesburg D4
Bath E4
Beaufort G6
Beech Island E4
Belton B3
Belvedere D4
Bennettsville B8
Berea B3
Bethune C7
Bishopville C7
Black Creek (creek) B7
Black Mingo Creek (creek) D9
Black River (river) D8
Blacksburg A4
Blackville E5
Bluffton G6
Bowling Green A5
Bowman E6
Branchville E6
Brandon B3
Brookwood k11
Broad River (river) C5
Brooklyn B6
Brunson F5
Bucksport D9
Buffalo B4
Bull Island G6
Bull Island G6
Bulls Bay (bay) F8
Calhoun Falls C2
Camden C6
Cameron D6
Campobello A3
Cape Island E9
Cape Romain National Wildlife Refuge E9
Capers Inlet (inlet) k12

Capers Island C3
Carlisle k11
Cat Island D4
Catawba River (river) D7
Cateechee E5
Cayce B2
Cedar Island E8
Central B4
Charleston B3
Chattooga River (river) F6
Chaw F7
Chesnee D9
Chester h12
Chesterfield k11
City View B5
Clark Hill Reservoir (reservoir) E5
Clearwater E5
Clemson D4
Clinton E4
Clio G6
Clover E4
Columbia B3
Columbia River (river) D4
Conestee B8
Congaree River (river) C7
Congaree Swamp National Monument B7
Converse B7
Conway D9
Cooper River (river) D8
Coosawhatchie River (river) A4
Cottageville E5
Coward G6
Cowpens A5
Cowpens National Battlefield E6
Cross Anchor E6
Cross Hill B3
Dalington k11
Daufuskie Island C5
Daw Island B6
Denmark F5
Denny Terrace B4
Dentsville G6
Dewees Inlet (inlet) B4
Dewees Island G6
Dillon B8
Donalds C2
Doneraile D6
Dorchester Estates C6
Drayton A3
Drum Island E9
Due West C2
Duncan E9
Easley k12

Eastover D6
Edgefield D4
Edisto Island F7
Edisto River (river) E6
Ehrhardt E5
Elgin R6
Elloree D6
Enoree River (river) B4
Estill F5
Eutawville E7
Fairfax F5
Fenwick Island k11
Fishing Creek (creek) B5
Fishing Creek Reservoir (reservoir) B6
Florence C8
Folly Beach F8
Folly Island F8
Forest Acres C6
Fort Lawn B6
Fort Mill A6
Fort Sumter National Monument F3
Fountain Inn B3
Francis Marion National Forest E8
Fripp Island G7
Gaffney A4
Gantt B3
Gaston D5
Georgetown E9
Giford E4
Gloverville E4
Gluck B3
Goose Creek F7
Goose Creek Reservoir (reservoir) F7
Graniteville D4
Gray Court B3
Great Falls B6
Great Pee Dee River (river) D9
Greeleyville D8
Greenville B3
Greenwood C3
Greenwood, Lake (lake) C4
Greer B3
Hampton F5
Hanahan F7
Hardeeville G5
Harleyville E7
Hartsville C7
Heath Springs B6
Hemingway D9
Hemlock B5
Hickory Grove A4
Hilda E5
Hilton Head Island G6
Hogback Mountain A3
Holly Hill E7
Hollywood F7
Honea Path B3
Hopkins C6
Horatio C7
Hunting Island G7
Hutchinson Island C4
Industrial A5
Inman A3
Intracoastal Waterway C10
Irmo C5
Isle of Palms F8
Iva C2
Jackson D4
Jacksonboro F6
James Island F8
Jamestown E8
Jefferson B7
Jeffries Creek (creek) C8
Jehossee Island F7
Jenkinsville C5
Joanna C3
Jocasee, Lake (reservoir) A2
Johns Island F7
Johnsonville D9
Johnston D4
Jonesville B4
Keowee, Lake (lake) B2
Kershaw B6
Kiawah Island F7
Kings Mountain National Military Park A5
Kingstree D8
Ladies Island G6
Ladson F7
Lake City D8
Lake Swamp (lake) C8
Lake View C9
Lamar C8
Lancaster B6
Lando B5

Landrum A3
Lane D8
Langley E4
Latta C9
Laurel Bay G6
Laurens B4
Leesville D4
Lemon Island G6
Lexington D5
Liberty B2
Lighthouse Inlet (inlet) k12
Lincolnville C7
Little Lynches River (river) C9
Little Pee Dee River (river) D3
Little River (river) D10
Little River Inlet (inlet) C9
Little Rock C10
Lowndesville C2
Loris C9
Lugoff C6
Luray B3
Lynchburg C7
Lynches River (river) D8
Manning D7
Marietta A2
Marion, Lake (lake) C9
Marion C9 *(Marion E7)*
Mauldin B3
Mayesville C7
McBee C4
McClellanville E9
McColl B3
McCormick D4
Midland Park k11
Monarch B4
Moncks Corner E7
Montmorenci D4
Morgan Island G6
Morris Island F8
Moultrie Lake (lake) E8
Mount Pleasant F8
Mullins C9
Murphy Island E9
Murray, Lake (lake) C5
Murrells Inlet D9
Murrells Inlet (inlet) D10
Myers D5
Myrtle Beach D10
Neeses D5
New Ellenton E4
Newberry C4
Newry B2
Nichols C9
Ninety Six B3
Norris B2
North A3
North Augusta D9
North Charleston D8
North Edisto River (river) E9
North Inlet (inlet) B4
North Myrtle Beach G6
North Santee River (river) D5
Norway D5
Olanta C9
Olar B3
Orangeburg B3
Otter Island k11
Wagener D7
Waterboro E7
Iva D7
Jackson B5
Pacolet Mills D10
Pacolet River (river) D5
Pageland C8
Palms, Isle of B3
Pamplico B4
Parkersville D4
Patrick D3
Pawleys Island B1
Pelham D7
Pendleton B4
Pickens D6
Pickney Island F5
Piedmont D4
Pinewood D9
Port Royal E5
Port Royal Island E6
Port Royal Sound (sound) E5
Price Inlet (inlet) B4
Pritchards Island m11
Prosperity B4
Ravenel B4
Reedy River (river) A4
Reevesville F8
Reidville F8
Ridge Spring C3
Ridgeland C6
Ridgeville D6

Ridgeway B4
Rock Hill B3
Rocky River (river) D3
Roebuck B7
Romain Cape E9
Rowesville E5
St. Andrews E6
St. Andrews E5
St. George B2
St. Helena Island B2
St. Helena Sound (sound) G6
St. Matthews B3
St. Phillips Island D7
St. Stephen G6
Saikehatchie River (river) G6
Salley k12
Saluda G6
Saluda River (river) C4
Sampit River (river) G6
Sandy Island k11
Santee River (river) C3
Sassafras Mountain E6
Savannah River (river) B3
Saxon D4
Scranton A5
Seabrook Island F6
Sellers B5
Seneca A3
Shannontown D8
Sharon E4
Shoals Hill Creek (creek) C9
Silverstreet G6
Simpsonville D4
Six Mile G6
Slater D5
Socastee B2
Society Hill k12
South Congaree C7
South Island C9
Spartanburg D3
Spring Island D10
Springdale C9
Springfield C10
Starr C6
Stono Inlet (inlet) C2
Stono River (river) C6
Sullivans Island B3
Summerton C7
Summerville D8
Sumter D7
Sumter National Forest A2
Surfside Beach F5
Swansea B4
Taylors F7
Timmonsville D8
Travelers Rest C9
Trenton E7
Troy B3
Tugaloo Lake (lake) D7
Turbeville C4
Tyger River (river) B3
Union B2
Valencia Heights A3
Varnville D9
Vaucluse D8
Waccamaw River (river) E9
Wadmalaw Island B4
Wagener G6
Waterboro D5
Walhalla D5
Ware Shoals C9
Wando River (river) B3
Wando Woods B3
Warrenville k11
Wateree Lake (lake) D7
Wateree River (river) E7
Wattsville D7
Waylyn B5
Welcome D10
Welford D5
West Columbia C8
West Pelzer B3
West Union B4
Westminster D4
Whitmire D3
Whitney B1
Williamston D7
Williston B4
Windy Hill D6
Winnsboro F5
Winnsboro Mills D4
Winyah Bay (bay) D9
Woodfield E5
Woodruff E6
Wylie, Lake (lake) E5
Yemassee B2
York B2

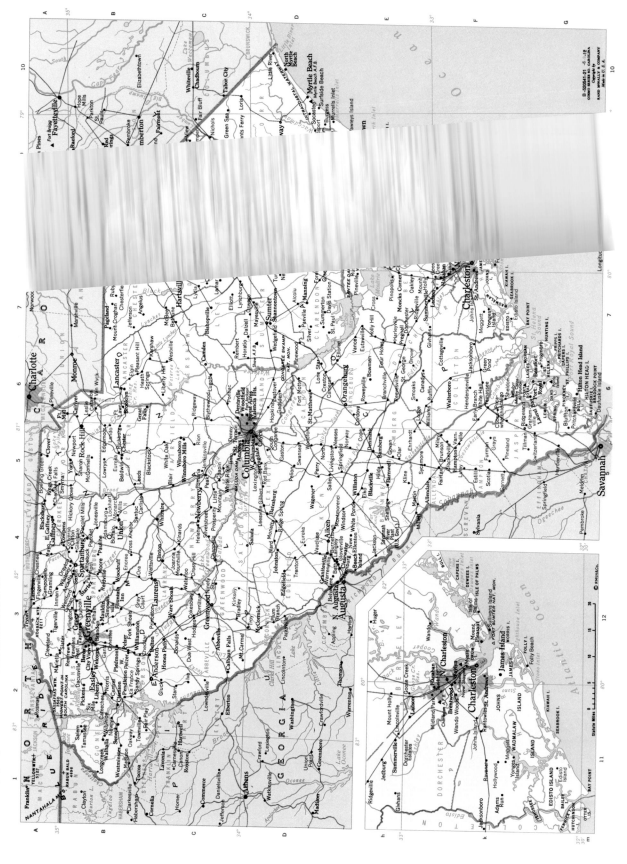

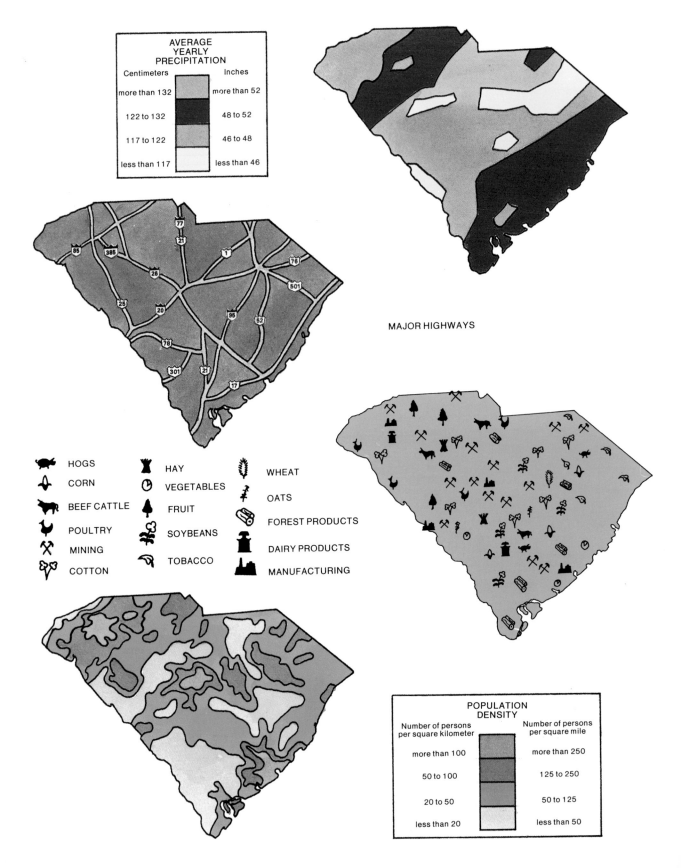

AVERAGE
YEARLY
PRECIPITATION

Centimeters		Inches
more than 132		more than 52
122 to 132		48 to 52
117 to 122		46 to 48
less than 117		less than 46

MAJOR HIGHWAYS

HOGS

CORN

BEEF CATTLE

POULTRY

MINING

COTTON

HAY

VEGETABLES

FRUIT

SOYBEANS

TOBACCO

WHEAT

OATS

FOREST PRODUCTS

DAIRY PRODUCTS

MANUFACTURING

POPULATION
DENSITY

Number of persons per square kilometer		Number of persons per square mile
more than 100		more than 250
50 to 100		125 to 250
20 to 50		50 to 125
less than 20		less than 50

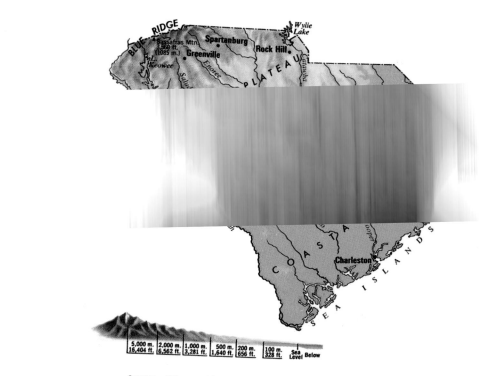

5,000 m. | 2,000 m. | 1,000 m. | 500 m. | 200 m. | 100 m. | Sea
16,404 ft. | 6,562 ft. | 3,281 ft. | 1,640 ft. | 656 ft. | 328 ft. | Level Below

COUNTIES

Cypress Gardens near Charleston

INDEX

Page numbers in boldface type indicate illustrations.

138

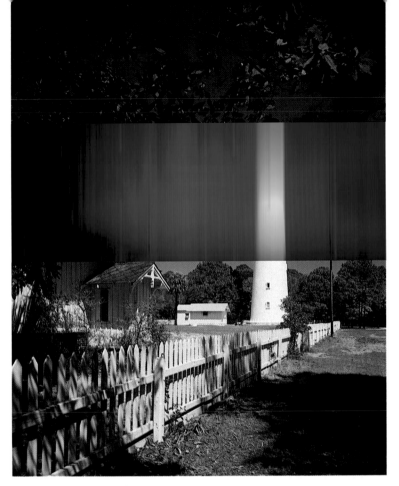

Picture Identifications

Front cover: Charleston
Back cover: Magnolia Gardens
Pages 2-3: Fishing on the Cooper River
Page 6: Charleston
Pages 8-9: A cypress swamp
Pages 20-21: Montage of South Carolina residents
Pages 26-27: An engraving of Charleston in 1739
Pages 42-43: An 1861 Currier & Ives lithograph of the bombardment of Fort Sumter
Page 60: A Steam-power plant in Georgetown
Page 72: The South Carolina State House in Columbia
Pages 80-81: A ballet performance during the 1984 Spoleto Festival U.S.A.
Pages 90-91: Oaks in South Carolina's coastal area
Page 108: Montage showing the state tree (Palmetto), the state flag, the state gemstone (amethyst), the state flower (Carolina jessamine), the state animal (white-tailed deer), and the state bird (Carolina wren)

About The Author

Deborah Kent grew up in Little Falls, New Jersey. She received a bachelor's degree in English from Oberlin College and obtained a master's degree in Social Work from the Smith College School for Social Work. After spending four years as a social worker in New York City, she moved to San Miguel de Allende, Mexico, where she began to write full-time. In addition to other books in the *America the Beautiful* series, she has written several novels for young adults.

Ms. Kent lives in Chicago with her husband and their daughter Janna.

Picture Acknowledgments

Front cover, © Steenmans/Zefa/H. Armstrong Roberts; 2-3, © Robert C. Clark; 4, © Robert C. Clark; 5, © Bob Glander/Shostal Associates/SuperStock; 6, © Eric Futran/The Marilyn Gartman Agency; 8-9, © Robert C. Clark; 11, © Robert C. Clark; 12 (left), © Max & Bea Hunn/Journalism Services; 12 (right), © Robert C. Clark; 13, © Robert C. Clark; 14, © Robert C. Clark; 15 (two photos), Robert C. Clark; 17 (top left, top right, middle right), © Robert C. Clark; 17 (bottom left), © Eric Futran/The Marilyn Gartman Agency; 17 (bottom right), SuperStock International; 19, © Robert C. Clark; 20 (middle right), © Michael Philip Manheim/The Marilyn Gartman Agency; 20 (top, bottom left), SuperStock International; 20 (bottom right), © Marsha Perry/Photo Options; 21 (top left), © Bill Barley/Photri; 21, (top right), © D.J. Forbert/Shostal Associates/SuperStock; 21 (bottom left), © Steve Price/Photo Options; 21 (bottom right), SuperStock International; 23, © Pat Abramson/Photo Options; 25, UPI/Bettmann Newsphotos; 26-27, The Granger Collection, New York; 30, The Granger Collection, New York; 33, The Charleston Museum; 35 (two photos), The Granger Collection, New York; 36, The Granger Collection, New York; 39, The Granger Collection, New York; 40, The Granger Collection, New York; 41, The Granger Collection, New York; 42-43, The Granger Collection, New York; 45, North Wind Picture Archives; 46 (two photos), The Granger Collection, New York; 48, The Granger Collection, New York; 50, The Granger Collection, New York; 51, The Granger Collection, New York; 52, Manuscripts Section, Howard-Titton Memorial Library, Tulane University, Louisiana Historical Association Collection; 53, Historical Pictures Service, Chicago; 54-55, North Wind Picture Archives; 56, The Granger Collection, New York; 57, North Wind Picture Archives; 59, South Carolina State Museum; 60, © Robert C. Clark; 63, The Bettmann Archive; 65, South Carolina State Museum; 67, South Carolina State Museum; 68, UPI/Bettmann Newsphotos; 72, © Robert C. Clark; 74, © Bill Barley/Photri; 76, © Robert C. Clark; 77 (right), © Robert C. Clark; 77 (left), Shostal Associates/SuperStock; 79, SuperStock International; 80-81, © William Struhs; 83 (left), © Virgina Grimes; 83 (right), The Bettmann Archive; 84 (left), The Granger Collection, New York; 84 (right), Museum of Fine Arts, Boston; 85 (left), Museum of Fine Arts, Boston; 85 (right), The Bettmann Archive; 87, © Pat Abramson/Photo Options; 89, © Norsingh/Photri; 90-91, © Robert C. Clark; 93 (map), Len W. Meents; 93, © Robert C. Clark; 95 (two photos), © Robert C. Clark; 96 (map), Len W. Meents; 96, Aiken Chamber of Commerce; 98 (two photos), © Robert C. Clark; 100 (map), Len W. Meents; 100, © Bob Costanzo, International Speedway Corporation; 101 (map), Len W. Meents; 101, © Robert C. Clark; 102, © Bill Barley/Shostal Associates/SuperStock; 103 (left), © Virginia Grimes; 103 (right), © Max & Bea Hunn/Journalism Services; 105 (top left), © D.J. Forbert/Shostal Associates/SuperStock; 105 (top right), © Michael Philip Manheim/The Marilyn Gartman Agency; 105 (bottom left), © James Blank/Root Resources; 105 (bottom right), © Eric Futran/The Marilyn Gartman Agency; 105 (bottom right), Cameramann International, Ltd.;107 (top), © Robert C. Clark; 107 (bottom left), © Bill Barley/Photri; 108 (flag), Courtesy Flag Research Center, Winchester, Massachusetts 01890; 108 (amethyst), © Louise K. Broman/Root Resources; 108 (palmetto), © Virginia Grimes; 108 (Carolina jessamine, deer), 108 (Carolina wren), © Helen Kittinger/Photo Options; 112, © Robert C. Clark; © Robert C. Clark; 115, SuperStock International; 117, © Virginia Grimes; 119, © W.D. Murphy/Shostal Associates/SuperStock; 120, © Monserrate J. Schwartz/Shostal Associates/SuperStock; 125 (Bethune), Historical Pictures Service, Chicago; 125 (Baruch), The Granger Collection, New York; 126 (Cunningham), Historical Pictures Service, Chicago; 126 (Conroy), AP/Wide World Photos; 126 (Butler), The Granger Collection, New York; 126 (Byrnes), The Bettmann Archive; 127 (Gadsden), Historical Pictures Services, Chicago; 127 (Hampton), The Bettmann Archive; 127 (Gibson, Gillespie), UPI/Bettmann Newsphotos; 128 (Hollings), AP/Wide World Photos; 128 (Heyward), Historical Pictures Service, Chicago; 128 (Kellogg), The Granger Collection, New York; 128 (Jackson), UPI/Bettmann Newsphotos; 129 (Mays, Peterkin), AP/Wide World Photos; 129 (Longstreet, Marion), The Bettmann Archive; 130 (Pickens), Historical Pictures Service, Chicago; 130 (Petigru, Pinckney, Poinsett), The Granger Collection, New York; 131 (Tillman, Timrod), Historical Pictures Service, Chicago; 131 (Watson), The Granger Collection, New York; 131 (Rutledge), The Bettmann Archive; 136 (map), Len W. Meents; 138, © Monserrate J. Schwartz/Shostal Associates/SuperStock; 141, © Gene Ahrens/Shostal Associates/SuperStock; Back cover, © Monserrate J. Schwartz/Shostal Associates/SuperStock

Metro Litho
Oak Forest, IL 60452

DATE DUE

TO GREAT EXPLORERS EVERYWHERE

ATHENEUM BOOKS FOR YOUNG READERS • AN IMPRINT OF SIMON & SCHUSTER CHILDREN'S PUBLISHING DIVISION

1230 AVENUE OF THE AMERICAS, NEW YORK, NEW YORK 10020 • TEXT COPYRIGHT © 2013 BY EILEEN ROSENTHAL • ILLUSTRATIONS COPYRIGHT © 2013 BY MARC ROSENTHAL • ALL RIGHTS RESERVED, INCLUDING THE RIGHT OF REPRODUCTION IN WHOLE OR IN PART IN ANY FORM. ATHENEUM BOOKS FOR YOUNG READERS IS A REGISTERED TRADEMARK OF SIMON & SCHUSTER, INC. • ATHENEUM LOGO IS A TRADEMARK OF SIMON & SCHUSTER, INC. • FOR INFORMATION ABOUT SPECIAL DISCOUNTS FOR BULK PURCHASES, PLEASE CONTACT SIMON & SCHUSTER SPECIAL SALES AT 1-866-506-1949 OR BUSINESS@SIMONANDSCHUSTER.COM. • THE SIMON & SCHUSTER SPEAKERS BUREAU CAN BRING AUTHORS TO YOUR LIVE EVENT. FOR MORE INFORMATION OR TO BOOK AN EVENT, CONTACT THE SIMON & SCHUSTER SPEAKERS BUREAU AT 1-866-248-3049 OR VISIT OUR WEBSITE AT WWW.SIMONSPEAKERS.COM. • BOOK DESIGN BY DAN POTASH • THE TEXT FOR THIS BOOK IS SET IN P22 POP ART • THE ILLUSTRATIONS FOR THIS BOOK ARE DRAWN IN PENCIL AND COLORED DIGITALLY. • MANUFACTURED IN CHINA • 0713 SCP • FIRST EDITION • 10 9 8 7 6 5 4 3 2 1 • ROSENTHAL, EILEEN. • BOBO THE SAILOR MAN! / EILEEN ROSENTHAL ; ILLUSTRATED BY MARC ROSENTHAL.—1ST ED. • P. CM. • SUMMARY: WILLIE FINDS ALL SORTS OF INTERESTING THINGS WHILE HE AND BOBO ARE EXPLORING, INCLUDING A BUCKET THAT WOULD BE A PERFECT BOAT FOR BOBO BUT BEFORE HE KNOWS IT, BOBO AND THE "BOAT" HAVE DISAPPEARED. • ISBN 978-1-4424-4443-0 (HARDCOVER) • ISBN 978-1-4424-4444-7 (EBOOK) • [1. ADVENTURE AND ADVENTURERS—FICTION. 2. LOST AND FOUND POSSESSIONS—FICTION. 3. TOYS—FICTION. 4. CATS—FICTION.] I. ROSENTHAL, MARC, 1949- ILL. II. TITLE. • PZ7.R7194455BOB 2013 • [E]—DC23 • 2012040456

BOBO

THE SAILOR MAN!

BY EILEEN ROSENTHAL

ILLUSTRATED BY MARC ROSENTHAL

ATHENEUM BOOKS FOR YOUNG READERS

NEW YORK   LONDON   TORONTO   SYDNEY   NEW DELHI

COME ON, BOBO, TODAY WE'RE GOING EXPLORING.

YOU KNOW, BOBO, EXPLORERS DISCOVER GREAT STUFF.
I THINK WE'RE GOING TO DISCOVER SOMETHING BIG,
LIKE DINOSAUR BONES OR A VOLCANO!

LOOK, MUSHROOMS!
POISON MUSHROOMS!

A FUZZY CATERPILLAR.
HE LIKES ME!

THIS IS A *PERFECT* EXPLORER STICK.

ZZZZOW!

A COMB.

SOME EXPLORER
MUST HAVE DROPPED THIS.

HEY, BOBO, LOOK AT THOSE CLOUDS.
THAT ONE LOOKS LIKE A BIG BOAT. . . .
AND THAT ONE LOOKS LIKE A SHARK!

LOOK, A RIVER!
AND A BUCKET!

WE CAN BE SAILORS!
OUR BOAT WILL BE RED AND WE CAN
BE FRIENDS WITH A SEA MONSTER!
HE'LL BE REALLY BIG.
BIG AND GREEN.

SPLASH
SPLASH

GET IN, BOBO.
NOW YOU'RE A SAILOR MAN!

HEY, DON'T GO TOO FAR.

BOBO! SLOW DOWN!

STAY THERE, BOBO.
I'M COMING.

UH-OH. THESE ROCKS ARE TOO SLIPPERY!
I CAN'T GET YOU.

BOBO, COME BACK.

DON'T BE SCARED, BOBO.
I'M COMING.

OKAY, I'VE GOT YOU!
HOLD ON TIGHT!

THUNK

BOBO! WE DID IT!

SAILOR MEN HAVE TO
WATCH OUT FOR ROCKS, BOBO.

LUCKY FOR YOU, I'M AN EXPERT FISHERMAN.

HEY, ARE YOU HUNGRY?

ME TOO.
LET'S GO HOME.

I NEED TO DRY YOU OFF.

BOBO, YOU HAVE TO FOLD IT JUST LIKE THIS. . . .

THESE ARE *OFFICIAL* EXPLORER HATS.
ONLY REAL EXPLORERS CAN WEAR THEM.
LIKE US!

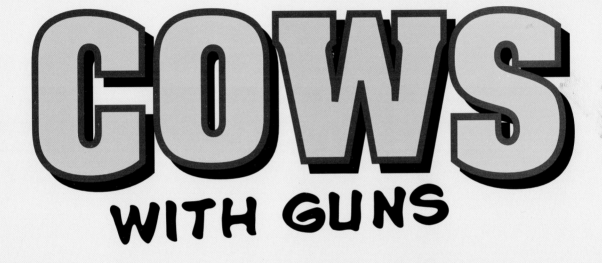

COWS
WITH GUNS

WRITTEN BY
DANA LYONS
ILLUSTRATIONS BY
JEFF SINCLAIR

PENGUIN
STUDIO

PENGUIN STUDIO
Published by the Penguin Group
Penguin Putnam Inc., 375 Hudson Street, New York, New York 10014, U.S.A.
Penguin Books Ltd, 27 Wrights Lane, London W8 5TZ, England
Penguin Books Australia Ltd, Ringwood, Victoria, Australia
Penguin Books Canada Ltd, 10 Alcorn Avenue, Toronto, Ontario, Canada M4V 3B2
Penguin Books (N.Z.) Ltd, 182–190 Wairau Road, Auckland 10, New Zealand

Penguin Books Ltd, Registered Offices:
Harmondsworth, Middlesex, England

First published in 1998 by Penguin Studio,
a member of Penguin Putnam Inc.

1 3 5 7 9 10 8 6 4 2

Copyright © Lyons Brothers Music (BMI), 1996, 1998
Copyright © Dana Lyons, 1998
All rights reserved

CIP data available

ISBN 0-670-87890-1

Printed in the United States of America
Set in future bold and comic demi
Designed by Jaye Elsie Zimet

Dedicated to the Memory of
Dana Lyons

For Karen, who paints in broad strokes and doesn't even know it.
—*Jeff Sinclair*

Dana would like to thank the following people for their love and support during this challenging "Year of the Bovine": Pat and Herb Lyons (Mom and Dad), Zach Lyons "Captain Boycott," Tim McHugh, Web Guru Aaron Booker, Ian Titley, Bay Renaud, and Punmeister Robbie Liben.

Also special thanks to Michael Fragnito, Laura Healy, Stacy Rockwood, and Jaye Zimet at Penguin Studio, and Peter Miller of PMA Literary and Film Management Inc.

COWS WITH GUNS performed by:
DANA LYONS: Guitars and Vocals
   With Mi Tierra Mariachi Band members:
ALBERTO LEYVA: Vihuela
RAFAEL LEYVA: Guitarron
JESUS SANCHEZ: Trumpet
BRETT LOVINS: Hawaiian Guitar on COWS WITH GUNS instrumental

... greasy breaded veal cutlet on the tray of some sophomore at UC Davis, placed him in a basket and set it in the Nooksack River, hoping that the Great Cosmic Cow would care for him. The basket floated out to Portage Island, in the Lummi Indian Reservation, where he was raised in secrecy by the cows there.

As a young calf, Cow Tse-Tongue couldn't get his hooves on enough political philosophy and military strategy books. Growing up on the reservation also allowed for easy access to fireworks. He became known as a nerdy veal who liked to play with explosives. Many town elders saw his gift and urged him to go visit the wild and famous Elinor Moosevelt on a pasture in northern Skagit County before he burned the whole island to the ground.

One night, he swam the channel and made his way down through the Chuckanut Mountains to the Skagit valley.

In short order he located Elinor and told his moving tail.

"You came to the right pasture, beefcakes. I've had it being treated like a piece of meat. It's time we round up the revolutionaries and hoof it on out of here. Hold on a second, Tongue, I'm going to get an old buddy of mine on the horn."

A few moments later Elinor handed him the phone. "Is that you, Tongue? Good to have you on board. I'm down here on the ranch outside of Fort Worth, Texas, raising food and working on the Bovine Bill of Rights. Hurry up and get your hide down here."

Elinor and Tongue piled into a 1949 Dodge pickup and headed south.

"In any revolution you need a cultured wordsmith who can spice up a speech and really get things cooking. . . someone with a good head for history who won't sell the rank and file out when victory is near. Thomas Hefferson is the bull we need to step to the plate."

Elinor and Tongue kept to the back roads, trying to avoid detection. Somewhere outside of Wichita they got pulled over next to a hog farm. "I never knew there were so many pigs in Kansas, Elinor. I hope this guy doesn't grill us too bad."

Cow Tse-Tongue got out of the truck.

"What's the beef, officer?"

"You were steering your car into the oncoming traffic. I wanted to make sure you hadn't spent too much time down at the watering hole. Let me smell your breath. Ooo. Cheesy. You're free to go."

Later that day they drove down a strip of gas stations, malls, and fast-food stops. Elinor spotted a gathering in front of a burger joint. "Try our new Rocky Mountain McOysters," the sign said.

"Who is that cute guy with the red hair, red boots, and little golden arches all over his happy suit?"

"Don't tell me that you're going to fall for that clown, Elinor. Just seeing that guy really grinds me up. Any idiot can see that he's full of baloney."

"Now, don't get jealous on me, Tongue, I'm just ribbing you."

"I'll show that clown a little bit about brand marketing."

Tongue jumped out of the truck and broke off the sizzling tailpipe from the truck's muffler. He pulled his orange NRA hat over his horns and picked his way through the crowd.

"Yes, we use every part of the cow here at the biggest burger joint in the world, that's why I know you'll enjoy our new extra-crispy deep-fried Rocky Mountain McOysters."

"Yo! Mr. Happy! You want your rings roasted or poached?!?"

A scream came from behind the clown, and Elinor dove over the stage, spraying the crowd with a five-gallon bucket of mustard. "Let's get out of here fast so they can't ketch up," Elinor yelled.

"You can't lose your temper like that, Tongue. You could have gotten us into a real pickle. I don't relish the idea of having my buns end up on their buns. Shake yourself out of it, man, or we'll both end up fried."

Back in the truck, speeding out of town, Cow Tse-Tongue calmed down. "I'm sorry, Elinor, there was something about that scene that really rubbed salt into the wound. It reminded me of the time my mother was hurting so bad on a milking machine, she had to be sent to the Mayo Clinic."

"I know," said Elinor. "Same thing happened to my sister Patti. It was udderly revolting."

Ten hours later they arrived at a ranch outside of Fort Worth. "That was a long drive. I hope this guy Hefferson was worth the trip."

They trotted back into a grove of mesquite trees and found an older steer surrounded by law journals, and by philosophy and history books.

"Elinor, so good to see you. And it's an honor to meat the great Cow Tse-Tongue. A prime cut. Hefferson's the name. Originally from Jersey."

"Jersey, you say? What exit?"

"I've been finishing up the Second Amendment, 'The Right to Arm Bears.' If we're serious in regaining our rightful place on the prairie and escaping our current position on the fast-food chain, we may need to enlist the help of other species."

"Brilliant, Hefferson, brilliant! Is that a stockyard across the highway?"

"Yes, I'm afraid it is, Tongue, and all those cows are slated to be hamburger tomorrow morning. And, Elinor, I'm sorry to say that your sister is among them."

"They caught Patti! My poor baby sister!"

"Easy, Elinor. Have no fear. Cow Tse-Tongue is here. Dry those lovely cow eyes of yours and grab that blowtorch."

Hefferson was uneasy. "But, Tongue, where will we go with five hundred head?"

"South of the border, Hefferson. There's a big mariachi festival in Nuevo León. I could die for a good margarita and those sweet violins."

With that, Hefferson, Moosevelt, and Tongue headed for the slaughterhouse gate. Hefferson hot-wired twenty semis while Elinor and Tongue herded the crew into the cattle cars. The cow convoy drove off into the night.

Thanks to the new trade agreement, the border crossing was a breeze. "Citizenship?" "Bovine." "How many of you?" "Five hundred and three." "Where are you going?" "The mariachi festival in Nuevo León." "Welcome to Mexico."

The festival was fabulous. Everyone was having a great time. Good food. Good drink. Outrageous music. Dancing all night.

Hefferson was just getting going on the importance of free speech and press in a democratic society when Fidel Cowstro showed up.

"Amigos, welcome to the party revolucionario." He glanced over at Elinor and smiled. "If I can't dance, I don't want to be in your revolution."

Cow Tse-Tongue grabbed his hoof. "Stunning performance on the trumpet, Fidel. What a set of lips."

Fidel offered everyone cigars. "So, I understand you are freedom fighters. What brings you to our grand fiesta?"
"We're looking for a national anthem for our movement. Needless to say, mariachi captures the hearts of bovines everywhere."

Fidel smiled. "I know a cat named Oliver who is a brilliant composer who won't do us wrong. Not only is he a great lyricist, he owns a Human who attempts to make a living as a folk singer. Oliver might be able to get his Human to sing our song. We can use him to get our message out amongst the two-leggeds."

"A Human singing a cow revolution song?"

"This guy will sing anything for a laugh and a free meal."

"Get him on the horn."

"Are you going to the Ungulate Military Strategy Conference in New Delhi, Tongue? You mustn't miss it. There are direct flights on Air India from Mexico City."

"Book us passage for five hundred and four head."

"I'll put it on my card." Fidel rushed off through the sea of mariachi enthusiasts to call his travel agent.

"What do you think of him, Elinor? I like his can-do attitude: the type of fellow who could hold off the largest military might in the world for four decades. And, can he blow that horn!"

"Have you seen anyplace to get some good grass around here, Tongue?"

"Follow me, my deer."

The flight to India was fabulous. Everybody was having a terrific time. The drinks ran out somewhere over Africa, and the only disappointment was that they were short a few vegetarian meals. Tongue and Fidel skipped dinner, trying to lose a few pounds to get in shape for the big stampede.

Their welcome to India was out of this world. "I love this country!" shouted Tongue. "They really know how to treat a cow in India. It's easy getting around on mass transit, and the Humans are terrific. At first I thought they were just trying to butter us up, but I'm telling ya, I could get used to this sacred-cow deal."

"I'll try to work something like that into our declaration of independence, Tongue."

"Good work, Hefferson."

At the hotel, Fidel reserved the penthouse suite for the party. Four hundred thirty-one local holy cows joined the crew for the hoedown. The lavish spread included the finest in vegetarian cuisine, traditional music, and world-class belly dancing. There was a small altercation when one of the spinach dishes came out with cheese in it, but this was quickly rectified.

"This place really knows how to service the herd," acknowledged Tongue.

"Grade-A prime choice, if you ask me," said Hefferson.

After the luncheon buffet, Cow Tse-Tongue gathered up the team. He was excited after an exhilarating self-empowerment workshop. "All the hardware we need to stock up for the rebullion is half off in the former Soviet Union. We leave in an hour. Book us train seats for nine hundred thirty-five, Fidel."

"I'll put it on my card."

No one expected the incredible scenery on the Trans-Siberian Railway. The Russian hospitality was fabulous. Everyone was having a great time. And the Russian reindeer, what a sense of humor! They drank a little too much and went a little overboard about beets and potatoes, but what a lovely herd.

Elinor, go gather the finest in the herd, the cream of the crop. I want them whipped into shape. Nothing half-and-half about it. There's only a two percent success in this mission, and I don't want anything going sour. If anyone gives you an icy response, we'll skim them off the top of the herd. We're going to milk this invasion for all that it's worth."

"That's fine with me, Tongue, but what if some whiz gives me a hard time? When they get scared, some of 'em can get a little jerky. Some of the crew are worried about getting creamed."

"Put 'em on ice and they'll cool off. Besides, backing out now is a moot point. I'm not in the mood to hear questioning of this movement. And, no loafing around. That sort of behavior really gets me stewed. All this anxiety reminds me of getting mugged on the New York strip."

"You butchered that joke, Tongue. What a punishment. Let's get back to work."

"That's kosher with me."

In order to avoid detection, Cow Tse-Tongue decided that the growing army would return to the U.S. via kayak. "Fidel, we're going to need one thousand, two hundred forty-one kayaks for the whole crew, now that three hundred and six reindeer have joined our ranks. And, thirty-five big outboards for those barges. And, two tugs. And, grain for everyone for a three-month trip. And, some nicely patterned matching tablecloths and napkins."

"I'll take care of it, Tongue."

"You know, Elinor, that guy has an amazing credit line for a notorious Communist revolutionary."

"It's the money he makes on the side from his trumpet playing, Tongue."

"Of course, of course, a true master."

They journeyed up along the Kamchatka and cut over the Bering Strait down along Alaska and into the inside passage, down to Vancouver Island.

"We'll slip across the border at nightfall and make our way to my home at Portage Island near Bellingham. We'll train there for several months and gather provisions. When we have reached full military readiness, we'll cross to the mainland and free my mom from the dairy. Then it is vital we deal the Humans a serious blow to their morale. We must take over and occupy one of their most treasured cities. A city of great artistic and cultural importance. Their majestic village on the hill. A thousand points of light. The crown jewel of American civilization. We will take. . . Omaha. After that, it's all gravy."

"Let us sing!"

"WE WILL FIGHT FOR
BOVINE FREEDOM,
AND HOLD OUR
LARGE HEADS HIGH.
WE WILL RUN FREE
WITH THE BUFFALO,
OR DIE."

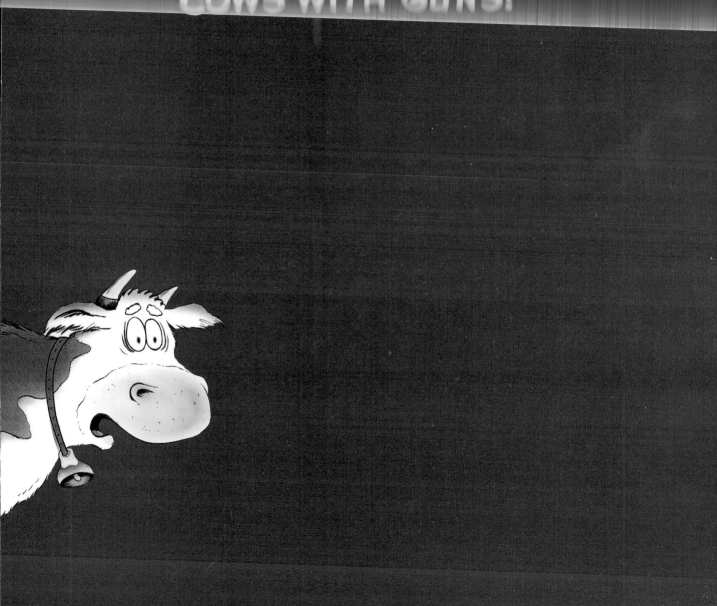

FAT AND DOCILE, BIG AND DUMB,
THEY LOOK SO STUPID,
THEY AREN'T MUCH FUN.
COWS AREN'T FUN!

THEY EAT TO GROW,
GROW TO DIE,
DIE TO BE ET
AT THE HAMBURGER FRY.
COWS WELL DONE!

NOBODY THUNK IT, NOBODY KNEW,
NO ONE IMAGINED THE GREAT COW GURU.
COWS ARE ONE!

HE HID IN THE FOREST,
READ BOOKS WITH GREAT ZEAL,
HE LOVED CHE GUEVARA,
A REVOLUTIONARY
VEAL.

BUT THEN HE WAS CAPTURED,
STUFFED INTO A CRATE.
LOADED ONTO A TRUCK,
WHERE HE RODE TO HIS FATE.
COWS ARE BUMMED!

BEEF ON BOARD

KNOCKED OVER A TRACTOR
AND RAN FOR THE DOOR,
SIX GALLONS OF GAS
FLOWED OUT ON THE FLOOR.
RUN, COWS, RUN!

GAS

HE PICKED UP A BULLHORN
AND JUMPED UP ON THE HAY,
"WE ARE FREE-ROVING BOVINES,

AND HOLD OUR LARGE HEADS HIGH.
WE WILL RUN FREE WITH THE BUFFALO,
OR DIE."
COWS WITH GUNS.

THEY CRASHED THE GATE
IN A GREAT STAMPEDE,
TIPPED OVER A MILK TRUCK,
TORCHED ALL THE FEED.

SIXTY POLICE CARS WERE PILED IN A HEAP,

BLACK SMOKE RISING,
DARKENING THE DAY,
TWELVE BURNING MCDONALD'S,
HAVE IT YOUR WAY!

THE PRESIDENT SAID,
"ENOUGH IS ENOUGH!
THESE UPPITY CATTLE,
IT'S TIME TO GET TOUGH."

BUT ON THE HORIZON,
SURROUNDING THE SHOPPERS,
CAME THE DEAFENING ROAR OF
CHICKENS IN CHOPPERS.

DANA LYONS was born in Kingston, New York. He now resides in Bellingham, Washington, and lives in a tree house with his cat, Oliver. One night in the summer of 1994, Dana was visited by the Great Cosmic Cow in a dream. He has not been the same since.

Dana has recorded five albums and wanders the globe searching for good swimming holes. He performs at clubs, schools, grange halls, and assorted ecological disaster areas.

JEFF SINCLAIR was born in Toronto and grew up in Surrey, British Columbia, Canada. Before being summoned by the mighty Cow Tse–Tongue and his melodic mastery, Jeff had illustrated more than thirty humorous books and received several local and international cartooning awards.

He spent several years as creative director for a national giftware company in Vancouver and has designed impulse products sold around the world. Jeff currently has no plans to run for office, run amuck, or da doo run run. He will continue to run free with the buffalo.